Practical Workouts for the School Theatre

by

Dorothy Hopkins Kirkland and Rehn Scarborough

Single copies of plays are sold for reading purposes only. The copying or duplicating of a play, or any part of play, by hand or by any other process, is an infringement of the copyright. Such infringement will be vigorously prosecuted

Baker's Plays
7611 Sunset Blvd.
Los Angeles, CA 90046
bakersplays.com

NOTICE

This book is offered for sale at the price quoted only on the understanding that, if any additional copies of the whole or any part are necessary for its production, such additional copies will be purchased. The attention of all purchasers is directed to the following: this work is fully protected under the copyright laws of the United States of America, the British Commonwealth, including Canada, and all other countries of the Copyright Union. Violations of the Copyright Law are punishable by fine or imprisonment, or both. The copying or duplication of this work or any part of this work, by hand or by any process, is an infringement of the copyright and will be vigorously prosecuted.

This play may not be produced by amateurs or professionals for public or private performance without first submitting application for performing rights. Royalties are due on all performances whether for charity or gain, or whether admission is charged or not. Since performance of this play without the payment of the royalty fee renders anybody participating liable to severe penalties imposed by the law, anybody acting in this play should be sure, before doing so, that the royalty fee has been paid. Professional rights, reading rights, radio broadcasting, television and all mechanical rights, etc. are strictly reserved. Application for performing rights should be made directly to BAKER'S PLAYS.

No one shall commit or authorize any act or omission by which the copyright of, or the right to copyright, this play may be impaired. No one shall make any changes in this play for the purpose of production.

Publication of this play does not imply availability for performance. Both amateurs and professionals considering a production are strongly advised in their own interest to apply to Baker's Plays for written permission before starting rehearsals, advertising, or booking a theatre.

Whenever the play is produced, the author's name must be carried in all publicity, advertising and programs. Also, the following notice must appear on all printed programs, "Produced by special arrangement with Baker's Plays."

Licensing fees for PRACTICAL WORKOUTS FOR THE SCHOOL THEATRE is based on a per performance rate and payable one week in advance of the production.

Please consult the Baker's Plays website at www.bakersplays.com or our current print catalogue for up to date licensing fee information.

Copyright © 1940 by Walter H. Baker Company
Copyright © 1968 (in renewal) by Clara Scarborough
Made in U.S.A.
All rights reserved.

PRACTICAL WORKOUTS FOR THE SCHOOL THEATRE
ISBN 978-0-87440-270-4
1199-B

Foreword

A good workman uses good tools. So does a good actor—the tools, in the latter case, however, being the mastery of certain fundamentals which, though technical, are not mechanical.

The young actor often reads about these fundamentals, hears his director discuss them, regards them for a time, perhaps, as a bit of theory—but straightway forgets all about them when he has a part to play.

Much rehearsal time would be saved, nervous energy conserved, and a finer performance given if all of the players who came to work had developed even a little skill in using some of the basic techniques of dramatic procedure.

The purpose of this book is to provide workshop material for learning a few of these techniques. It is addressed to the young, inexperienced, high school student, who, though not expecting to make the theatre his profession, nevertheless is not satisfied with the awkward, slipshod absurdities which at one time characterized the average school play; to students who have not yet acquired a background knowledge of classical drama, and for whose use the sophisticated Broadway play is inappropriate.

Due to increasingly advanced standards, the term "amateur" has taken on a new meaning. Whereas it once signified crudity and self-exploitation on the stage, it has, in recent years, come to imply a progressive effort toward truth, sincerity, and integrity in theatre practise, being now an expression of commendation rather than otherwise. In colleges, universities, and civic groups, this new distinction is well known. Everywhere, high schools are striving for a higher calibre of dramatic work expressed in choice of plays, polish in acting, and smoothness in production.

It is with the hope of helping serve these standards that this volume has been prepared. Each scene is a complete dramatic unit and, while directed toward exercise in a specific problem, may be made to cover several at once. Development of skill should be accumulative—accomplishment in one lesson carried on and applied in the next situation regardless of the technical point being emphasized at the moment. Only when this plan is maintained does the " whole become greater than the sum of its parts."

The workshop method of presentation, employing no scenery, no costumes, no properties, is not only splendid training in that it concentrates the imagination on the acting and the theme, but it is really entertaining and interesting. Actors themselves have always known this. Broadway has just found it out. Truly, " The art of the theatre may be a state of mind, not a building." To believe, with William Butler Yeats, that " my theatre must be the ancient theatre made by unrolling a carpet, or marking out a place with a stick, or setting a screen against a wall," or with Hallie Flanagan that " the theatre is a place where an idea is so ardently enacted that it becomes the belief of actors and audiences alike," is to discover a new, fresh thrill in all dramatic work.

CONTENTS

1. **ENTRANCES AND EXITS** 7

    Elizabeth Refuses.....Scene 1. 1m. 3w. (From "Pride and Prejudice.") By Margaret Macnamara . . 9
    Elizabeth Refuses.....Scene 2. 1m. 4w. By Margaret Macnamara . 14
    A Mad Breakfast..... 3m. 6w. By Isabel M. Grey . . 17

2. **GROUPING** 23

    The Inspector-General..........8m. By Nikolai Gogol . . 25
    Monsieur Beaucaire............8m. 7w. Dramatized from Booth Tarkington's story by Ethel Hale Freeman . 28
    Little Women.................5w. Dramatized from Louisa Alcott's story by Roger Wheeler . . . 33

3. **CROSSES AND TURNS** 40

    The Cherry Orchard......... 5m. 5w. and extras. By Anton Chekov . . 42
    Lady Windermere's Fan......Scene 1. 1m. 3w. By Oscar Wilde . 50
    Lady Windermere's Fan......Scene 2. 1m. 3w. and extras. By Oscar Wilde . . 52
    The Psychological Moment....Scene 1. 2w. By Patricia Morbio 54
    The Psychological Moment....Scene 2. 2w. By Patricia Morbio 57

4. **TRANSITIONS** 60

    Eether or Eyther..............2m. 2w. By R. C. V. Meyers . 61
    The Lean Years...............1m. 1w. By Mary Katherine Reely . 67
    The Wild Duck...............1m. 2w. By Henrik Ibsen . . 70

5. **MOTIVATION** 75

    Trifles ....Scene 1. 2w. By Susan Glaspell 76
    Trifles ....Scene 2. 2w. By Susan Glaspell 78
    A Heart Too Soon Made Glad. 3m. 2w. By Warren Beck 82
    The Maid of Domrémy....... 1m. 1w. By Joe Corrie . 88

6. **STAGE BUSINESS** 93

    The Kelly Kid............. 1m. 4w. By Kathleen Norris and Dan Totheroh . 95
    Pygmalion and Galatea..... 1m. 1w. By W. S. Gilbert . 102
    What Men Live By.......Scene 2. 2w. Adapted from Tolstoi's story by Virginia Church . . 106

7. **MISCELLANEOUS BUSINESS** 109

    Mary the First............. 1m. 1w. By Rachel Crothers . 111
    Glamour .... 2m. 1w. By Percival Wilde . 115
    The Affairs of Men........Scene 1. 2m. By Warren Beck . 117

CONTENTS

8. SPEAKING CONVERSATIONALLY 123

   Grandma Pulls the String..Scene 1. 3w. By Edith B. Delano and David Carb . . 124
   Grandma Pulls the String..Scene 2. 2w. By Edith B. Delano and David Carb . . 127
   Grandma Pulls the String..Scene 3. 1m. 1w. By Edith B. Delano and David Carb . . 129
   The Wedding Present......Scene 1. 1m. 1w. By William Carson . 132
   The Wedding Present......Scene 2. 2m. 1w. By William Carson . 135

9. TEMPO AND CLIMAX 137

   What Men Live By........Scene 1. 1m. 1w. Adapted from Tolstoi's story by Virginia Church . . 138
   Riders to the Sea.......... 1m. 3w. By J. M. Synge . 140
   The Affairs of Men........Scene 2. 2m. By Warren Beck . 144
   Catherine Parr............. 1m. 1w. By Maurice Baring . 147
   The Short Cut............. 2m. By Percival Wilde . 149
   When the Sun Rises....... 1m. 2w. By Dorothy C. Allan 152

10. RADIO BROADCASTING 158

    Not Quite Such a Goose......2m 2w. By Elizabeth Gale. Adapted for the radio by Roger Wheeler . 159
    The Gold Bug—Tales from Poe. 4m. Adapted for the radio by Frederick Garrigus . 163

Entrances and Exits

To get on and off the stage properly is not as simple as it appears. Badly done, the actor places himself at a disadvantage and mars the play.

There is no deviation from the rule: *Both entrances and exits must be made on time and in character.*

An entrance or exit which is not well timed will lose effect, spoil the rhythm of the play and cause a serious let-down. The doorways must be cleared to avoid any awkwardness and each character must know exactly when to go on and off.

A center entrance is most striking, but any upstage entrance, making a diagonal movement toward center, is effective. Except when antecedent action requires different handling, the entering character should not linger near the door, but walk well into the scene, establish himself, and then speak.

In making an exit, start with the upstage foot and go off quickly. Do not dawdle as it causes an anticlimax and holds everybody up. The character should be as near the exit as possible before actually going out. In "breaking an exit with a speech," he goes to the door on the concluding speech, pauses to speak the final words, then turns and goes out. The remaining actors must not let the scene sag after an exit. Both entrances and exits should be well knit or there will be big holes in the play.

An entrance and exit should be built up by the lines and business of the other people in the play, or, in some types of plays, by the employment of off-stage effects such as thunder and lightning, hoofbeats, motor sounds, shouts from crowds, the opening of a door slowly or suddenly,— and many other similar devices suitable to the situation.

Off-stage conversation (which is a part of the play), before an entrance or after an exit, should be planned.

Never try to ad lib. If sufficient lines are not provided in the play, make up others.

From the first moment an actor is visible, until the time he is actually out, he must create the illusion of the character he is playing. He cannot do this if he has been talking and laughing off stage just before going on. During these moments he must exercise all of his powers of concentration and imagination, thinking the thoughts and evoking the emotions of the person he is supposed to be. By starting his entrance several paces back from the door so that his movement has gained full momentum, he can better give the impression that he has actually come from the place suggested in the play, rather than having waited in the wings for his cue. A similar method should be used in making an exit, walking off a little distance past the door, taking care not to slow down while in sight of the audience.

*ELIZABETH REFUSES

(Scene 1)

From Jane Austen's "Pride and Prejudice"

BY MARGARET MACNAMARA

SCENE.—*The morning-room at the Bennett's. The essentials are an exit* L. *to the library and another* R. *to the hall, both upstage.*

CHARACTERS: ELIZABETH BENNETT.
JANE BENNETT.
MRS. BENNETT.
MR. COLLINS.

(ELIZABETH *enters from the library, armed with a large book. She sits down in the armchair and starts to read. She finds it difficult to concentrate and lapses into sad thought.* JANE *enters, also armed with a book from the library, and this spurs* ELIZABETH *to assiduous reading.* JANE *sits and opens her book, but notices that her sister is wiping away a tear, and is about to speak when the appearance of* MRS. BENNETT *from the hall brings both girls to their feet— such was the deference paid to elders in Jane Austen's days.*)

MRS. BENNETT. (*Fretfully*) What are you at, you girls? (*They show their books and she continues.*) I should think you might find some more agreeable occupation when you know my nerves are all upset. (*She drops into the armchair* ELIZABETH *offers.*)

JANE. Can I fetch you anything, mamma? Your smelling salts?

* Copyright, 1926, Joseph Williams, Ltd.

Elizabeth. A fan?

Mrs. Bennett. Don't be fidgety, girls,—sit down, do. It was bad enough to have to look forward to your father's death with the certainty that we should be turned out of house and home! To be forced to receive the heir as our guest and entertain him for untold ages!

Elizabeth. A clergyman's week, mamma.

Jane. Ten days are passed.

Mrs. Bennett. I wonder Mr. Collins had the impertinence to ask for an invitation! *We* didn't want to make up the family quarrel. He comes here—a perfect stranger—all hypocrisy—professing his goodwill—and eyeing every piece of furniture as if he were to inherit it of right, instead of by that monstrous entail.

Elizabeth. But, mamma, Mr. Collins *has* the right—"entail" merely means that the inheritance is in the male line. If one of us had been a boy ——

Mrs. Bennett. Oh, la, Lizzy, your father has explained the entail to me a thousand times. But that makes no difference! It's an iniquitous affair—and he ought to have done something about it, instead of leaving me a widow with five daughters, and not a penny to support them beyond the two hundred a year he got with me!

Jane. (*Very gently*) Mamma, may we not find comfort in the fact that dear papa is in excellent health, and but fifty years of age?

Mrs. Bennett. Don't nag at me, Jane! I hate the sight of Mr. Collins! He's walking around the park now, hugging himself at the thought that it will soon be his—and not the least ashamed of the entail!

Elizabeth. *We* have no liking for Mr. Collins, mamma, but if only you would try to understand that the entail is as lawful as ——

Mrs. Bennett. (*Interrupting*) Don't dare to teach me, Lizzy! A nice reward for sparing you for a long visit to your aunt and uncle! Ungrateful girl, I looked for a very different outcome of your holiday! But young men seem to be as scarce in other neighborhoods as they are round us. In all the while you were away from home, did you receive one eligible offer?

Elizabeth. N-no.

Mrs. Bennett. I never supposed you would! There's not one of you in the way of obtaining a husband except Jane. She's my sole consolation. As I was saying the other day to Lady Lucas, " Jane is provided for. We shall soon see Jane keeping house in the handsomest mansion in this part of the country."

Jane. (*Rising*) Dear mamma, I have no such expectation!—at least ——

Mrs. Bennett. Oh, Jane, what an untruth! Isn't he forever at your side? Didn't he offend Lady Lucas's daughter by dancing four times with you, and never once asking her? Tell me that, miss!

Elizabeth. Mamma, we may guess at intentions—*I* think them obvious—but to have them spoken of—especially outside the family—it distresses Jane unspeakably!

Mrs. Bennett. So I'm to ask your leave to speak, am I? I'll not stay here to be sauced!

Elizabeth. (*Rising towards her*) I beg your pardon, mamma. I didn't ——

Jane. Believe me, mamma, I know it is in kindness ——

Mrs. Bennett. (*With an air of dignity*) Stand aside, both of you! I am going to the housekeeper's room, to give the morning's orders. (*Dropping her dignity for querulous complaint.*) They ought to have been done an hour ago, but my poor nerves are in such a flutter —— (*She pauses.*)

Jane. Might I give the orders for you, mamma?

Mrs. Bennett. (*Dignified again*) No, I thank you! I don't want any interference in *my* house. If you want to please your mother, take a little more pains to get an establishment of your own. *I* can't provide for you when we are all thrown out of doors by that wicked, wicked entail! (*She has talked herself off into the hall.*)

Jane. (*Ruefully*) Mamma means *so* well by us!

Elizabeth. (*Moving down* L. *and not looking at* Jane) I have the advantage over you in one thing, Jane —she knows nothing of my unfortunate affairs.

Jane. It *was* awkward for you that she asked whether you had received an eligible offer.

Elizabeth. (*Turning*) Why "awkward"?

JANE. Mr. Darcy is very handsome, very rich, and of high birth and breeding. His station is much above ours.

ELIZABETH. (*Sitting*) At the time I did not think him eligible in character.

JANE. Oh, I ought to have understood! You rejected Mr. Darcy because you did not love him.

ELIZABETH. (*Looking away from* JANE) I rejected him because I was foolishly prejudiced by that lying tale in which he figured as mean, disloyal, revengeful! Now I have the satisfaction of knowing that I refused the most generous and upright of men.

JANE. (*Behind* ELIZABETH'S *right shoulder*) Poor Lizzy! But—in the circumstances—would it not be wise to remember your own early impressions of his character? (*Moves away to* C., *then looks at* ELIZABETH.) Before that false report reached your ears I have heard you speak strongly against his pride. (ELIZABETH *can find no answer.* JANE, *after a slight pause, crosses and sits down.*) Ah, well, perhaps Mr. Darcy may renew his proposal.

ELIZABETH. (*Energetically*) Never! He *is* proud! He said, himself, he loved me against his will. *Once* love conquered pride, and he stooped to a woman beneath him in social standing. *Twice* is unthinkable.

(MRS. BENNETT *returns, talking.*)

MRS. BENNETT. Girls! Here is Mr. Collins back from his walk already! *You* must entertain him! My nerves are not equal to a single word! (*Sits down heavily.*)

(JANE *and* ELIZABETH *shoot to their feet at the word* "*Girls.*" JANE *crosses to* ELIZABETH. MR. COLLINS *bows in the entrance.*)

MR. COLLINS. If I may be pardoned the intrusion, dear ladies, I should be gratified by permission to sit in your company.

MRS. BENNETT. Oh, la, Mr. Collins, you are welcome to sit here and chat, but you must excuse *me* from taking any part. I have the headache.

(*He bows and advances.*)

JANE. Won't you be seated, Mr. Collins? (*Pointing to chair.*)

MR. COLLINS. (*Bowing*) I thank you! I thank you sincerely! (*He bows, fetches chair and sits* C.) I am always glad to converse with ladies. (*He clears his throat.*) Your father, my dear cousins, has just apprised me of a very pleasing circumstance. He is acquainted—I understand the family is acquainted—with Mr. Darcy, who is the nephew of my patroness, Lady Catherine DeBurgh. It seems that Mr. Darcy has stayed in this neighborhood!

MRS. BENNETT. I've no opinion of Mr. Darcy. He shewed himself far too high and mighty to please my daughters. If he is your Lady Catherine's nephew, I hope she has better manners than him.

MR. COLLINS. The minutest concerns of *all* her neighbors are of interest to Lady Catherine. She has even condescended to advise me to marry. On that topic, however, I do not propose to enlarge until Mrs. Bennett is relieved of her headache, and an opportunity arises of broaching it in private.

MRS. BENNETT. (*Excited*) What do you say, sir? Girls, it is high time you took the air! Go out for a walk!

(*They rise; so does* MR. COLLINS.)

MR. COLLINS. (*Bowing*) I should be gratified if they would honor me—that is to say—if Miss *Jane* would honor me by remaining within call.

MRS. BENNETT. Oh, as for Jane—but that does not signify. (*Rises.*) I will explain —— You had better both remain within call. (*Crossing to them.*) Go into the library—your father won't mind. (*They curtsey to her and go.* MR. COLLINS *moves up as if to open the door, putting the chair away as he goes. They incline their heads to his bow.*) Pray be seated, Mr. Collins. Take the settee.

(*With a bow, he seats himself in the middle of it.*)

Mr. Collins. If your headache is too severe, dear Mrs. Bennett, I will ——
Mrs. Bennett. (*Interrupting*) Oh, la, that's gone off! . . .

*ELIZABETH REFUSES

(Scene 2)

From "Pride and Prejudice"

by Margaret Macnamara

SCENE.—*Same as Scene 1.*

Characters: ELIZABETH BENNETT.
JANE BENNETT.
MRS. BENNETT.
MR. COLLINS.
LADY CATHERINE DeBURGH.

(Elizabeth *has just rejected* Mr. Collins' *proposal of marriage. She is seated, and as he shows no intention of leaving, she rises.*)

Elizabeth. There is but one way to cut short our conversation. (*She sweeps across the room and out into the hall.*)
Mr. Collins. (*Bowing as she passes him*) Ultimately, I am persuaded, my proposals will not fail to be acceptable.

(*She has gone. He turns front with a smirk and moves* l.)

Mrs. Bennett. (*Speaking off stage*) Lizzy, where are you going? Silly girl! (*Entering.*) Well, Mr. Col-

* Copyright, 1926, Joseph Williams, Ltd.

lins, we won't mind her! Let me be the first to congratulate you!

MR. COLLINS. My most cordial thanks, dear Mrs. Bennett! By and by, I trust, Miss Elizabeth will be as ready as I am to receive your congratulations! I flatter myself that her refusal of my addresses was the reverse of serious!

MRS. BENNETT. Refuse you—did she?

MR. COLLINS. With all the apparent firmness of a truly elegant female!

MRS. BENNETT. Oh, dear, this will never do! (*Hastening to the doorway. He struts across the stage.*) Lizzy! Come back! Come back, I say! I'll bring her to reason! Lizzy! (ELIZABETH *returns.*) Come right in! (ELIZABETH *obeys.*) Looking as unconcerned as may be! Caring for nothing and nobody but to get your own way! What's this Mr. Collins tells me? You have rejected him?

ELIZABETH. Yes, mamma.

MRS. BENNETT. You are a foolish, headstrong girl, and do not know your own interest! But I will *make* you know it! I insist upon your ——

MR. COLLINS. (*Astounded*) Pardon me for interrupting you, madam, but can your exhortations be necessary?

MRS. BENNETT. That they are, Mr. Collins! She has always been a handful to control! Lizzy, I insist upon your marrying Mr. Collins! He is most obligingly doing what he can to make amends for that wretched entail, and you presume to set up your obstinate will against those who ——

MR. COLLINS. (*Interrupting*) Pardon me again, madam, but if she is *really* headstrong and foolish—I know not whether she would be a very desirable wife for a clergyman like myself!

ELIZABETH. Indeed I should not, Mr. Collins!

MRS. BENNETT. You would, you naughty girl! Mr. Collins, you misunderstand—Lizzy is only headstrong in such matters as these. In everything else she is as good-natured a young woman as ever lived. I will go directly to Mr. Bennett, and we shall soon settle it with her.

(*Moving toward library and calling.*) Mr. Bennett,—you must come and make Lizzy marry Mr. Collins! She vows she will not have him—(*off, screaming*)—and if you do not make haste he will change his mind and not have *her!* (*Returning.*) Oh, dear, he's not in the library. I'll speak to him on the first opportunity!

Mr. Collins. Pray do not be at the trouble, Mrs. Bennett! If my cousin persists in rejecting my suit, I feel it might be better not to force her to accept it.

Mrs. Bennett. Nonsense, Mr. Collins! She shan't defy her parents like this!

Mr. Collins. (*Interrupting*) Pardon me once more, madam! Pardon me! I cannot help fearing that she *has* defects of temper—and independence of spirit—that would not contribute to my felicity.

Elizabeth. I know I should make you miserable!

Mrs. Bennett. Oh, Lizzy, how can you tell such a falsehood?

Elizabeth. And offend Lady Catherine!

Mrs. Bennett. Be quiet, miss!

Mr. Collins. Enough, Mrs. Bennett! Allow me to withdraw my proposals! (*She collapses into armchair.*) In so doing I mean no disrespect to you, nor shall I resent your daughter's behavior. . . . I will now, by your leave, retire to my room to compose my sermon for the coming Sunday. [*Bows and goes out through hall.*

Mrs. Bennett. Oh, you are tiresome, Lizzy! Ten to one he is too put out to give you another chance.

Elizabeth. I am sorry to vex you, mamma.

Mrs. Bennett. You know you are nothing of the sort! I am in a dreadful state! I tell you what it is, Miss Lizzy, if you take it into your head to go on refusing every offer of marriage, you will never get a husband at all! (Jane *slips in.*) Jane! You'd better talk to Lizzy. I can do nothing with her! She's been trampling on poor Mr. Collins without the smallest regard for my feelings. (*Loud knock.*) There's a knock at the front door. If it's your father come back, I shall fetch *him* in to you—then we shall see! [*Departs, talking.*

Jane. Mercifully, you are not afraid of papa.

Elizabeth. What would mamma say if she knew of

my earlier offer? (*Throwing herself on settee, arms out along the back.*) Oh, Jane, how ridiculously I am punished for my prejudice against Darcy! You should have heard how Mr. Collins rejected my repeated refusals! He couldn't believe in my annoyance! Little did he guess that the sting of it lay in my bitter certainty that Darcy will never ask me again! I don't know whether to laugh or cry!

JANE. My dear, dear Lizzy! From my heart I pity you.

(MRS. BENNETT'S *voice is heard, off. She appears in doorway.*)

MRS. BENNETT. This way, Lady Catherine! (*She ushers* LADY CATHERINE *in.*) Girls, the knock was Lady Catherine DeBurgh! My daughters, Lady Catherine.

(JANE *is on* ELIZABETH'S *right. The girls curtsey.*)

*A MAD BREAKFAST

BY ISABEL McREYNOLDS GREY

SCENE.—*The breakfast room of a modest boardinghouse. Two tables, each set for four. Door from hall. Door to kitchen. Serving table near kitchen entrance. Small table with mail, newspapers, etc., near hall entrance.*

CHARACTERS: MRS. SIMPKINS.
LIZZIE.
MISS BROWN.
MISS SMITH.
MISS GREEN.
MRS. HILL.
MR. HILL.
MR. ROBERTS.
MR. JONES.

* Copyright, 1929, Walter H. Baker Company

(*As the curtain rises,* Mrs. Simpkins *is discovered laying forks and knives on one table. Enter* Lizzie *from kitchen, with a tray of cups and saucers.*)

Mrs. Simpkins. About time to ring the bell, isn't it?
Lizzie. Not for five minutes yet.
Mrs. Simpkins. You'd better ring it. They're always late anyway. [*She goes off to the kitchen.*

(Lizzie *sighs and arranges the cups and takes up a huge bell. She goes to the hall, ringing the bell. Enter from the hall,* Miss Brown *and* Mr. Jones. *The bell stops.* Mr. Jones *picks up a letter, which he opens.* Miss Brown *looks toward tables, sees the breakfast is not served, takes up a newspaper and glances at it.* Mr. Jones *reads his letter and laughs as he reads.*)

Miss Brown. Well, what is so amusing?
Mr. Jones. (*Starts to speak but stops to laugh*) It's too good to keep. I'll have to share it!
Miss Brown. What?
Mr. Jones. (*Waving the letter*) This!
Miss Brown. Has someone left you a fortune?
Mr. Jones. Read it! (*Handing her the letter.*)
Miss Brown. (*Reading*) "Mr. Jones, Dear Sir: Shall arrive at the institution as soon after six-thirty as possible. Thanking you for providing me with this opportunity for observation and study, I am" . . . (*To* Mr. Jones.) What does this mean?
Mr. Jones. It's a hoot! It means that we're going to have the time of our young lives —— (*He takes a newspaper clipping from his pocket and hands it to her.*)
Miss Brown. (*Reading*) "A middle-aged, well-to-do gentleman of excellent social position would like to visit a small, select, private home for the insane, for the purpose of investigation and study. Any information will be gratefully appreciated and well paid for. Address communications to . . ." (*Her voice trails off in amazement.*)
Mr. Jones. Isn't it rich!
Miss Brown. You don't mean to say ——

Mr. Jones. I do. I answered his ad and he answered my answer—sounds like Gilbert and Sullivan—but that's the truth.

> (*The bell rings furiously. Conversation is hopeless. They gaze at the ad and the letter until the bell stops.*)

Miss Brown. But where did you send him? His letter says——

> (*Before he can reply there is a last furious peal of the bell and* Lizzie *enters from the hall. She crosses toward the kitchen door.*)

Mr. Jones. Good-morning, Lizzie.
Lizzie. (*Mournfully*) Good-morning.
Mr. Jones. Have you finished the novel yet?
Lizzie. No. I'm just on the last chapter. It's awful sad.
Miss Brown. What is the title of the novel?
Lizzie. "United in Death." It's awful sad.
Miss Brown. I'll lend you a good story. It's called "All for Love," and it ends happily.
Lizzie. I like the sad ones best, thank you. They seem more natural.   [*Exits to kitchen.*

> (*Enter* Miss Smith, Mr. Roberts, Mr. *and* Mrs. Hill. *General "Good-mornings" and a search for mail at the side table. The Hills take places at the table furthest from the hall door.* Mr. Roberts *is seated at the other table.* Mr. Hill *reads the morning paper and* Mr. Roberts *gazes morosely at the bare table-cloth.* Miss Brown *sits at the table with the* Hills. Lizzie *enters with tray of glasses of fruit juice which she places, exits to kitchen and returns with the coffee. Enter* Mrs. Simpkins, *going to the table at which* Mr. Roberts *is seated.* Mrs. Simpkins, *after a general "Good-morning," pours the coffee which* Lizzie *serves after she has placed various dishes on each table, from which the guests*

help themselves. MR. JONES *detains* MISS SMITH *near the hall door.*)

MR. JONES. Good-morning, Miss Smith!
MISS SMITH. Perhaps it is a good morning, Mr. Jones, but to one of my temperament, morning is a simply inhuman part of the day. To me,—day doesn't begin till about one P. M.
MR. JONES. You should be an actress, Miss Smith.
MISS SMITH. Don't I know it? I'm acting all the time! I've got so much temperament that sometimes the very sight of a typewriter makes me want to scream!
MR. JONES. I wonder you don't leave the office. Go on the stage. I'm sure you've got talent.
MISS SMITH. Mr. Jones, I've got genius—though perhaps you'll think I shouldn't say it about myself—I *know* it! My friends all claim that my voice has the same timbre and a much more sympathetic quality than Ethel Barrymore's!
MR. JONES. You'd better look out. Some of these managers will snap you up one of these days.
MISS SMITH. Why, that's just the trouble, Mr. Jones. I've never met one.
MR. JONES. You can't say that very long.
MISS SMITH. How's that?
MR. JONES. Oh—(*waving his hand airily*)—nothing. But—you ought to be prepared is my advice —— (*A gesture indicating " the world is yours for the taking."*)

(MISS SMITH *dazedly takes her place at the table with the* HILLS *and* MISS BROWN.)

MRS. SIMPKINS. (*Who has been serving breakfast*) Aren't you coming to breakfast, Mr. Jones?
MR. JONES. I—ahem! . . . I'm waiting for someone. May I say a word, Mrs. Simpkins? Pardon me, folks. (*He crosses to* MRS. SIMPKINS, *leans over and whispers. She starts, but he restrains her by placing his hands firmly on her shoulders. Then, observing* MISS GREEN *entering, says very brightly.*) Ah, here's Miss Green!

(Miss Green *enters from hall, in painter's smock.* Mrs. Simpkins *rings for* Lizzie, *who comes in from kitchen.* Mrs. Simpkins *gives her an order in an inaudible tone.*)

Lizzie. (*Who has been listening with growing amazement*) Yes, mum! [*Returns to kitchen.*

Mr. Jones. (*Continuing a conversation with* Miss Green) You work all the time!

Miss Green. I know I do,—but the light was so good! I think this portrait is going to make my fortune—I really do!

Mrs. Simpkins. (*Elaborately sarcastic*) I suppose old Tony, the peanut man, will buy it to hang in his front parlor!

Miss Brown. Oh, really, Mrs. Simpkins, we all wish Miss Green success, I'm sure!

Miss Green. But Mrs. Simpkins is right. Tony is a good subject, but not a good purchaser. Now, if I could only find a millionaire with an interesting face, who would let me paint it——

Mr. Hill. (*Emerging from newspaper*) They go to the beauty parlors for that. Haw! (*He gets under cover again.*)

Mr. Jones. (*Detaining* Miss Green *as she is about to take her place at* Mrs. Simpkins' *table*) Just a word in confidence, Miss Green. (*His voice drops and he goes on inaudibly but uses pantomime to put over his points.*)

Miss Green. I never heard of him!

Mr. Jones. Never heard of him! Excuse me, please. (*Whispers long and emphatically.*)

Miss Green. (*Slowly*) I see. He might give me an order for a portrait. Thank you! (*Coldly.*) I hope I am not yet reduced to that sort of deception!

Mr. Jones. My mistake! I beg your pardon! I thought you might be interested!

Mrs. Simpkins. And *when* may we expect—your *friend*, Mr. Jones?

Mr. Jones. Any moment now. I think I'll look out for him. [*Goes out through hall door.*

(*Everyone else registers inquiry and surprise.*)

Copies of the complete plays from which these scenes are made can be supplied by the publishers

Grouping

Grouping does not consist solely of people posed in a static picture. It is a scene in flux—fluid, changing—with an ever balanced contour.

Except for a court function, avoid the formal, theatric, rigid arrangement of a center entrance with the characters lined up on each side, or a crowd massed into amphitheatre effect.

Grouping must: (1) produce a pictorial effect, (2) emphasize the psychological relationship of the characters, and (3) provide a focal point as a center of interest.

What form will most nearly accomplish these requisites? Experiment for a moment. Arrange a number of people in a circle, a semicircle, a straight line. Note how, in each case, the group is uninteresting, no relationship is expressed, and all the characters seem of equal importance. Rearrange them into the form of a triangle and note how, instantly, the group develops a center of interest, a dramatic relationship, and how it becomes a plastic form lending itself to smooth readjustment.

The triangle, then, becomes the basis for the composition of stage pictures. Since the stage is no longer considered a mere platform, but conceived as three dimensional, this principle is carried further. *Triangular composition means also this formation achieved in a plane either oblique or perpendicular to the floor;* that is, an arrangement of characters in such a way that lines drawn from the heads of each character to the others would form a triangle. This is accomplished by characters in a combination of standing and seated positions, or by the employment of levels, as steps, platforms, ramps, etc.

The apex of the triangle (which is the center of interest) may be that point which is nearest the floor or the one which is farthest from the floor; it may be one person or a group of people; and it may occur upon any area of the stage,—not necessarily the geometrical center.

In grouping, remember, also, that it is possible to make a play pleasing to the eye as well as significant.

Do not hesitate to try new variations; the possibilities are limitless.

*THE INSPECTOR-GENERAL (REVIZOR)

BY NIKOLAI GOGOL

Translated and Adapted by
John Dolman, Jr.
and
Benjamin Rothberg

SCENE.—*A room in the home of the Town Governor. Main entrance, with double doors, up* R. *Doors down* R. *and up* L.

CHARACTERS: ARTEMI PHILIPPOVICH ZEMLYANIKA, *the Director of Welfare.*
AMMOS FYODOROVICH LYAPKIN-TYAPKIN, *the Judge.*
LUKA LUKICH KHLOPOV, *the Superintendent of Schools.*
STEPAN ILYICH UKHAVYORTOV *the Police Captain.*
CHRISTIAN IVANOVICH HUEBNER, *the German doctor.*
SVISTUNOV, *a police orderly.*
DERZHIMORDA, *another police orderly.*
ANTON ANTONOVICH SKVOZNIK-DMUKHANOVSKY, *the Town Governor.*

(*As the curtain rises, the Judge, the Superintendent of Schools, the Doctor, and the Captain of Police are exchanging greetings, and asking in some excitement why they have all been summoned to the Governor's house so early in the morning.* SVISTUNOV, *the*

* Copyright, 1937, Walter H. Baker Company

Governor's orderly, ushers in the Director of Welfare, who is the last to arrive. All speak at once.)

ZEMLYANIKA. Good-morning, gentleman. What is it all about?

LYAPKIN-TYAPKIN. We don't know. Anton Antonovich has called us together. He hasn't appeared . . .

KHLOPOV. (*Interrupting*) Good-morning. We haven't seen the Governor yet.

ZEMLYANIKA. (*At the same time*) Who else is summoned?

UKHAVYORTOV. (*To* HUEBNER, *in a lower tone, at the same time*) Whatever it is, Christian Ivanovich, they'll blame us for it.

HUEBNER. Ja, ja.

UKHAVYORTOV. But we didn't do it.

HUEBNER. Nein.

ZEMLYANIKA. Are they all here?

LYAPKIN-TYAPKIN. All but Ivan Kuzmich, the Postmaster.

KHLOPOV. He hasn't finished sorting the letters.

ZEMLYANIKA. Reading them, you mean.

UKHAVYORTOV. It's probably something trifling after all.

HUEBNER. Ja.

UKHAVYORTOV. So early in the morning too.

(*All this has been very rapid and simultaneous. Now the Town Governor appears hurriedly from another room,* L., *preceded by* DERZHIMORDA, *another orderly, who steps aside and salutes and then disappears* R.)

ANTON ANTONOVICH. Good-morning. . . . Good-morning, gentlemen. My apologies. My apologies for calling you together so early. But I have just received a very unpleasant piece of news!

LYAPKIN-TYAPKIN. What?
ZEMLYANIKA. News? News?
KHLOPOV. You hear that?
HUEBNER. Wass?
UKHAVYORTOV. Sh! Listen.

(*Simultaneously. They converge upon him.*)

ANTON ANTONOVICH. An Inspector-General is coming!
LYAPKIN-TYAPKIN, A Revizór?
ZEMLYANIKA. An Inspector-General?
HUEBNER. Wass?
(*Simultaneously.*)

ANTON ANTONOVICH. Yes. A Revizór from Petersburg. And what is worse, he's coming *incognito!*
KHLOPOV. *Incognito!*
UKHAVYORTOV. From Petersburg! Incognito!
(*Simultaneously.*)

ANTON ANTONOVICH. And I understand he has *secret instructions!*
ZEMLYANIKA. Secret instructions!
LYAPKIN-TYAPKIN. (*Choking and clearing his throat*) Good Heavens!
ZEMLYANIKA. We've been lucky so far, but it's our turn now!
KHLOPOV. (*To the Judge*) My gosh! Secret instructions!
ANTON ANTONOVICH. I had a premonition of it last night. I dreamt I saw two enormous rats. They came snooping about and then . . . prrrrr . . . (*they all start*) vanished! This morning: a letter from Andrei Ivanovich Chmikov. You know him, Artemi Philippovich. I'll read it. He says . . . er . . . (*Mumbles over first part of letter.*) " My dear friend . . . er . . . I have much news for you . . . among other things . . ." —Ah, here it is!—" I must warn you that a government inspector has been detailed to visit your district, with secret instructions to pay particular attention to your town!"
KHLOPOV. Our town!
LYAPKIN-TYAPKIN. Good Lord!
ZEMLYANIKA. Particular attention!
(*Simultaneously.*)

ANTON ANTONOVICH. (*Continuing*) "This I have from trustworthy sources, but I hear also that he is travelling *incognito,* posing as a private gentleman. So, my dear friend, if you have any little faults that won't bear inspection . . . you are a practical man, I know, and in public affairs there are many harmless little forms of graft . . . (*he pauses significantly; all look self-conscious, and the Judge coughs*) er . . . if you have any little faults, I advise you to be careful, for this Revizór may appear at any moment! Indeed, he may be there already, staying somewhere incognito. (*All show panic.*) Yesterday my cousin and her husband " . . . er . . . but the rest of it is about family matters. Now! What do you think of that?

*MONSIEUR BEAUCAIRE

A Dramatization of Booth Tarkington's Novel

BY ETHEL HALE FREEMAN

ACT I. SCENE 2.—LADY MALBOURNE'S *house. The essentials are a door, up* C., *and doors* R. *and* L.

CHARACTERS: LADY MALBOURNE.
ESTELLE.
MARIE.
LADY BARING-GOULD.
LADY RELLERTON.
LADY MARY.
LADY CLARISE.
WINTON.
HARRY RACKELL.
LORD TOWNBRAKE.
MR. BANTISON.
SIR HUGH GUILFORD.
MR. MOLYNEUX.
CAPT. BADGER.
BEAU NASH.

(LADY MALBOURNE *stands* D. R. C.; ESTELLE *on her* R., MARIE, D. R., WINTON, *the butler,* U. C.)

*Copyright, 1916, Ethel Hale Freeman

WINTON. (*Announcing*) Mr. Harry Rackell.
LADY MALBOURNE. What, Harry! Ah, we heard you had returned from France.
HARRY. Do you not observe my Parisian pirouette?
LADY MALBOURNE. Dear boy! You are quite dazzling—surely. Welcome once more to Bath.
HARRY. Will you not greet me as kindly, Estelle?
ESTELLE. Do not come to me for compliments until I have observed you quite thoroughly.
HARRY. Oh, your pardon. I had forgot you had entered the ballroom of fashion. Dear me—you are quite—quite a lady, I see.
ESTELLE. Sir!
HARRY. (*Sighing*) Alas! Will you never again race me over the lawn, or play castle on the wall? But, Madam, you will, at least, permit me to paint you.
LADY MALBOURNE. Indeed, yes, Harry. You need not pout, Estelle, for you know very well that your hair and color will never be better.
ESTELLE. (*Laughing*) Now is not that a gloomy observation, friend Harry? But so it goes, does it not? No sooner may one enter the gay ballroom than lo! the music stops. Oh, yes, paint me at once, or teach your art to transcend the ugly.
HARRY. Let us begin, then, at once, (HARRY *and* ESTELLE *move* L. C. *together*) before youth cools down and the ruthless grip of time —— (BEAU NASH *appears* U. C. *where he crosses* L. *to* R.; HARRY *sees him and stops abruptly.*) Bah!—cease emotions. I am cut off by a wapping fop. (ESTELLE *laughs.* LADY MALBOURNE *frowns in disapproval.*) What a perfect doll is our Beau, a powdered, exquisite rosette—no, a captious poppy bobbing on its stem!
ESTELLE. Take care, Harry. Mother will place a keen eye on your manners tonight.
HARRY. "Madam Mother" shall be rewarded—you shall see me when the pompadours arrive. No one shall match me for velvet and elegance!
ESTELLE. Softly, Harry. Mother, you know, believes you are vastly clever; be careful not to arouse her attention or she will discover how really dull you can be.

(LADY MALBOURNE *is giving directions to* MARIE.)

HARRY. Nonsense, Estelle. It is quite impossible for me to be dull. Besides, since leaving England, I have looked on things which would startle music in a stone. I have seen ——

LADY MALBOURNE. What have you seen, young Harry?

HARRY. Such painting, Madam!

LADY MALBOURNE. Ah, indeed!

HARRY. (*Crossing* C.) Through the courtesy of our Ambassador, I was permitted to enter the Galerie Royale where some new paintings were hung—by a great French master, though yet scarcely known. There was one—it was of a young prince ——

LADY MALBOURNE. My dear Harry, I applaud your fervor, but ah, excuse me—Winton, set more lights in the second card-room. Marie, the ladies who arrive in chairs will be conducted to the reception speciale.

ESTELLE. (*Sweetly*) Harry, you may tell *me* about the portraits. Come into the conservatory.

HARRY. Gladly. (*They start out door* L.)

WINTON. Lord Townbrake!

HARRY. (*After one glance over his shoulder at* TOWNBRAKE) Just in time. It's unpardonable for an English lord to possess a face like his! [*They laugh and go out.*

TOWNBRAKE. Ah, Lady Malbourne, your servant. Is it possible I am here before Nash? Ah, I forgot, he appears *after* we are gathered—to make a sensation, of course. Quite so.

WINTON. Mr. Bantison, Lady Clarise.

(*Enter* BANTISON, LADY CLARISE *and* MOLYNEUX *following.*)

LADY MALBOURNE. (*With evident pleasure but not losing her dignity*) My dear child, delighted. And is not Mr. Molyneux to come also?

MOLYNEUX. But two steps behind, Lady Malbourne. Think you it would be prudent for me to entrust my young cousin to this foolish Bantison? My compliments, Madame.

BANTISON. What's that, Molyneux?

LADY MALBOURNE. He says you are not a safe escort for Lady Clarise. Fie, Mr. Bantison!

BANTISON. Eh? Ha, why no—ah—of course—you know—I vow I should run away with her on the spot; ha, ha!

LADY CLARISE. How witty you are, Mr. Bantison. Now who but you could do such a thing as "run away on the spot"?

BANTISON. Eh?—ah—ah—I don't follow—ah.

WINTON. Beau Nash.

(BEAU NASH *enters pompously* U. C., *and at once assumes a place of importance* R. C.)

ALL. Ah!

BEAU NASH. My compliments, Lady Malbourne. Good-evening, all.

LADY MALBOURNE. My dear Beau, pray tell me, are the colors right—and the ferns, do say that the ferns are——

BEAU NASH. (*Very seriously*) Ah—too bright a green at the mirror, and a trifle dark in yonder retreat. Otherwise—ah—very well; yes, I may pronounce it very well done.

LADY MALBOURNE. Oh, I am so happy! And will you not correct the order of the dance? (*Hands him a paper.*)

BEAU NASH. (*With great importance*) Ah, yes, certainly—at once. Hm! Harry Rackell—who is he? (*He and* LADY MALBOURNE *start downstage.*)

LADY MALBOURNE. A young artist, just returned from Paris.

BEAU NASH. Hm—ah——

LADY MALBOURNE. He has been presented at the Assembly at Lyons.

BEAU NASH. Ah, that will do. Of course one must make sure of these little matters.

TOWNBRAKE. Eh? Rackell? Is he back? Clumsy young cur; hope he's improved.

LADY CLARISE. Have you ever tried the Paris cure, Lord Townbrake?

TOWNBRAKE. Eh? What? What Paris cure?

LADY CLARISE. Mr. Rackell's. Come, Mr. Bantison, you may lead me through the rooms. [*They go off* L.

MOLYNEUX. I do not see your charming daughter, Lady Malbourne.

LADY MALBOURNE. She is relieving the room of Harry's crude manners—there—beyond.

MOLYNEUX. Ah, giving him a few finishing touches. I'll plead for a lesson, as well —— [*Exit*, L.

BEAU NASH. And who is to lay claim to the Beauty of Bath? Winterset, no doubt?

LADY MALBOURNE. I believe Lady Mary is to favor Mr. Molyneux tonight. (*A trifle disturbed.*) The Duke is less prompt than usual.

WINTON. Sir Hugh Guilford, Captain Badger, Lady Baring-Gould. (*Enter the same;* TOWNBRAKE *crosses to* D. L. C.) Lady Rellerton, Lady Mary Carlysle.

(*A silence; the men watch eagerly.* MOLYNEUX *appears at door*, D. L., *bringing two other ladies. Enter* LADY RELLERTON *and* LADY MARY, U. C. *A silence. All turn and bow profoundly; then group nearer* LADY MARY.)

BEAU NASH. (*To* LADY MALBOURNE) I think we may allow the musicians to begin.

(LADY MALBOURNE *signals to* WINTON, *who motions to musicians, off* U. L. *A few notes sound from an adjoining room.* SIR HUGH *and* BANTISON *move with ladies toward door* R.)

*LITTLE WOMEN

From a new Dramatization of
Louisa M. Alcott's Book

BY ROGER WHEELER

SCENE.—*The sitting-room in the Marches' home in Concord, Massachusetts, five o'clock in the afternoon of the day before Christmas, 1863. The room is a large, old-fashioned sitting-room typical of the Civil War period. This scene centers around the fireplace, near which is a large, comfortable easy chair with arms.*

CHARACTERS: MEG.
JO.
BETH.
AMY.
MRS. MARCH.

(*The four March sisters are discovered as the curtain rises.* MEG *is sitting in the easy chair, sewing.* JO *is awkwardly seated on a hassock by the fire.* BETH *is seated at the organ [or piano] almost unseen in that dark part of the room, playing a Christmas carol very softly.* AMY *is sitting at the R. of the easy chair, on the floor near* MEG'S *feet. She has a small drawing-board and pencil and is sketching.*)

JO. (*Pokes at the fire*) Christmas won't seem like Christmas without any presents, will it, Meg?

MEG. (*Busy with her sewing*) I don't suppose it will, Jo. (*Rests sewing in her lap, looks forlornly at her dress and sighs.*) Oh, dear! It's so dreadful to be poor!

AMY. (*Petulantly as she sketches*) I don't think it's fair for some girls to have plenty of pretty things—and other girls nothing at all.

JO. Oh—I say now, Amy! I don't think you should say " we've nothing at all."

AMY. (*With a toss of her head*) Well, I mean——

* Copyright, 1934, Walter H. Baker Company

BETH. (*Suddenly stops playing*) Jo's right, Amy!

AMY. (*Turns to* BETH) 'Course you'd side with Jo, Beth—you always do. Just the same—what have we for Christmas? A dollar each from Aunt March! Pooh!

BETH. (*Turns on stool and faces others. Quietly*) We've got Father and Mother and each other, Amy.

AMY. (*A bit taken aback*) Oh,—well, I meant ——

Jo. We haven't got Father, Beth—and we shan't have him for a long time. (*With a sudden burst of spirit.*) Oh—wish I was a man and could be off fighting the Rebels!

BETH. (*Timidly*) Do you mind if I stop playing now? It's cold over here and ——

Jo. Aren't we the selfish ones? Sitting cosily here by the fire and letting Beth freeze at the organ. (*Rises and crosses to* C.) Here—you sit on the hassock, Beth. I'll sit on the floor.

BETH. (*Rises and crosses* L. *Gives* Jo *an affectionate little hug as she passes her*) Thank you, Jo! (*Sits on hassock and warms her hands by fire.*) My, it's nice and warm here.

(Jo *sprawls on the floor* L. C. *near* AMY.)

MEG. (*Sews again*) You know the reason Mother doesn't want us to have any presents this year, Jo? It's going to be a hard winter for everyone, and she thinks we ought not to spend money for pleasure, when our men are suffering so in the army. We can't do much, but we can make some sacrifices, and we ought to do it gladly. (*Sighs.*) But I'm afraid I don't.

Jo. But, Meg—I don't think the little we'd spend would do any good. We've each got a dollar—and the army wouldn't be helped much by our giving that. I agree not to expect anything from Mother or you girls—but I *do* want to buy " Undine and Sintram " for myself. I've wanted it *so* long!

BETH. I planned to spend mine for new music.

AMY. (*Decisively*) Well, I shall get a nice box of Faber's drawing pencils. I really need them.

Jo. Mother didn't say anything about our money. She won't want us to give up everything.

AMY. (*Approvingly*) That's right, Jo!

Jo. (*Sits up and hugs her knees*) Let's each buy what we want and have a little fun. We work hard enough to earn it. Don't you think we do, Meg?

MEG. I know *I* do—teaching those tiresome King children nearly all day, when I'm longing to enjoy myself at home.

Jo. Humph! You don't have half such a hard time as I do——

MEG. (*Quickly*) Is that so, Jo March? Well, I'll have you understand——

Jo. How would you like to be shut up for hours with a nervous, fussy old lady, who keeps you trotting and worries you till you're ready to fly out of the window?

BETH. Well, I think washing dishes and keeping things tidy is the worst work in the world.

MEG. (*Turns to* BETH *in surprise*) Why—Beth! I thought you liked housework.

BETH. (*Examining her hands*) It makes my hands stiff and I can't practice my music well at all.

AMY. I don't believe any of you suffer as I do. *You* don't have to go to school with impertinent girls, who plague you if you don't know your lessons, and laugh at your dresses, and label your father because he isn't rich, and——

Jo. If you mean *libel*, Amy, I'd say so—and not talk about labels, as if Papa was a pickle-bottle.

AMY. (*Indignantly*) I know what I mean, Jo March—and you needn't be *statirical* about it!

Jo. (*Laughs*) *Statirical!*

AMY. That's what I said! It's proper to use good words—and—and—improve your *vocabilary*.

Jo. It's not voca*bil*ary—it's voca*bul*ary!

AMY. (*Hotly*) That's what I said!

Jo. You didn't, Amy March!

AMY. I did, too! (*Defiantly to* Jo.) Anyway, I don't use slang and whistle like you do.

Jo. That's because you can't whistle. Listen to me! (*Starts whistling " Yankee Doodle."*)

AMY. I wouldn't want to—it's too boyish!

Jo. (*Stops whistling*) That's why I do it.

Amy. I detest rude, unladylike girls!

Jo. Well, I hate affected, niminy-piminy chits!

Meg. (*Reprovingly*) Now—now! Josephine! Amy!

Jo. Well, I don't care, Meg! I can't get over my disappointment in not being a boy! It's worse than ever, now. I'm dying to go and fight with Papa—but I have to stay home and knit like a poky old woman!

Beth. (*Sympathetically*) Poor Jo! It's too bad—but it can't be helped.

Meg. (*Turns to* Amy) As for you, Amy—you're altogether too particular and prim. You'll grow up an affected little goose, if you don't take care. I like your nice manners and refined ways of speaking, when you don't try to be elegant—but *your* absurd words are as bad as Jo's slang.

Beth. (*Meekly*) If Jo's a tomboy and Amy a goose—what am I, Meg?

Meg. (*Tenderly*) You? You're a dear, Beth—and nothing else.

Jo. (*Suddenly turns and looks at the clock*) Christopher Columbus! It can't be after five o'clock already!

Meg. (*Rises*) It is! Marmee'll be home any minute. (*Crosses to table and puts down sewing.*) Amy, move Marmee's chair up near the fire! (Amy *rises—puts drawing-board away. Moves the easy chair nearer the fire.*) Jo—you warm her slippers!

Jo. (*Rises*) All right, Meg! I'll toast 'em good and hot. (*Gets* Marmee's *slippers under the sofa—brings them down to fire and warms them.*)

Beth. (*Rises*) What can I do, Meg?

Meg. Fix the hassock for Marmee's feet!

(Beth *arranges the hassock in front of easy chair.*)

Jo. Look at these slippers, girls! (*Holds out slippers.*) They're almost worn out. Marmee ought to have a new pair.

Beth. I thought I'd get her some with my dollar.

Amy. (*Sits on the arm of easy chair*) No, Beth—I shall!

Meg. (*At the table*) I'm the oldest ——

Jo. (*Warms slippers again at the fire*) No! I'm the man of the family now Papa is away—*I* shall provide the slippers. Father told me to take special care of Mother while he was gone.

Beth. (*Crosses to* L. C. *eagerly*) I tell you what we'll do! Let's each get Marmee something for Christmas—and not get anything for ourselves.

Jo. (*Enthusiastically*) Topping!

Meg. (*Sits in chair* L. *of table*) Good for you, Beth.

Amy. What'll we get?

Meg. (*Thoughtfully*) Well—I shall get her a nice pair of gloves.

Jo. (*Promptly*) Slippers from me.

Beth. Handkerchiefs—all hemmed.

Amy. I'll get a little bottle of cologne. Marmee likes it—and it won't cost much, so I'll have some money left to buy my pencils.

Meg. How will we give the things?

Jo. Put them on the table here, Meg, and bring Marmee in and see her open the bundles. Don't you remember how we used to do it on our birthdays?

Amy. We can let Marmee think we're getting the things for ourselves—and then surprise her.

Jo. Good idea, Amy! We'll have to go into the village after supper to shop—but I don't think Marmee'll mind. She ——

(*Door slams off stage* R.)

Meg. (*Rises*) Sssh! There's Marmee now!

Jo. (*Warningly*) Quiet—everyone! Don't let her suspect!

(Marmee *enters arch at back.* Marmee *is a quiet, attractive-looking woman of about forty. She is neatly dressed in clothes suitable to the period. She has on a bonnet and shawl. As she enters, all four girls rush to greet her. She kisses each in turn.*)

Marmee. Hello, my girls! How have you got on today?

Meg. Fine, Marmee!

Jo. Great!

Amy. I had the best mark in school today.

Beth. Everything's all right here, Marmee. Hannah's getting supper.

Meg. Here—let me take your bonnet! (*Unfastens* Marmee's *bonnet, goes off* L. *to put it away and re-enters.*)

Amy. I'll put your shawl away, Marmee! (*Takes shawl and repeats* Meg's *action in putting it away.*)

Jo. (*Leads* Marmee *to easy chair*) Here are your slippers all hot, Marmee! (*Picks up slippers from fireplace.*)

Beth. Let me unfasten your wet shoes, Marmee!

Marmee. (*Sits in easy chair as girls flutter about to arrange for her comfort*) Well, well, isn't this cosy? Has anyone called, Beth?

Beth. No, Marmee.

Marmee. Jo, you look tired to death. Now, come—all of you! (*Girls gather round.*) Sit down! I've got a treat for you.

Amy. (*Excitedly*) I know—I know! A letter!

Meg. (*Sits on right arm of chair*) A letter from Father?

Jo. (*Shouts*) Hurrah! Three cheers for Father!

Beth. What does it say, Marmee?

Marmee. (*Takes a letter from the pocket of her dress*) Yes—a nice long letter from your father.

Amy. (*Sits on left arm of chair*) I'm just dying to hear it.

Jo. (*Goes to back of chair and leans over*) Read it, Marmee!

Marmee. Now, now! Have patience! It's a nice long letter. Father says he is well, and thinks he shall get through the cold season better than we feared. He sends all sorts of loving wishes for Christmas, and a special message for you girls.

Jo. A message for us? Oh—read that first!

Marmee. (*Finds place in letter*) " Give my girls my dear love and a kiss. Tell them I think of them by day, pray for them by night, and find my best comfort in their affection at all times. A year seems very long to wait before I see them, but remind them that while we wait we may all work, so that these hard days may not be wasted. I know they will remember all I said to them, that they will be loving children to you, will do their duty faithfully, fight their bosom enemies bravely, and conquer themselves so beautifully, that when I come back to them I may be fonder and prouder than ever of my little women." (*After a short pause in which girls sob a little.*) There!

AMY. (*With a sob*) I *am* a selfish girl! But I'll truly try to be better, so he mayn't be disappointed in me by and by.

MARMEE. (*Tenderly*) That's my Amy.

MEG. I think too much of my looks, and hate to work—but I won't any more, if I can help it.

MARMEE. (*Softly*) Meg!

JO. I'm going to try to be what Father loves to call me—" a little woman "—and not be rough and wild.

MARMEE. Beth, wouldn't you like to play something—for Father?

BETH. (*Rises and crosses to organ* [*or piano*]) Of course I will, Marmee! What shall I play?

JO. I know! I think we all ought to sing " My Country 'Tis of Thee." Father's fighting for our country and—I think it would please him.

MARMEE. (*Rises*) That's a good idea, Jo.

(MARMEE, JO, MEG *and* AMY *cross and group themselves around* BETH.)

JO. Ready, Beth!

(BETH *plays " My Country 'Tis of Thee " softly and they all sing as the curtain falls.*)

Copies of the complete plays from which these scenes are made can be supplied by the publishers

Crosses and Turns

The questions which arise here are: Who? When? How? Briefly and in general, these are the answers.

The one in whom the dramatic interest is centered initiates the cross. Sometimes, when two actors are standing in a " line " position, it is necessary for the other character to make a slight readjustment of position by a simple counter-crossing. For example:

A is, dramatically, the center of interest. He makes a cross down stage left, passing B.—B simultaneously readjusts his position by a " counter " cross in another direction.

The length of the cross and the counter-cross is determined by the intensity of the thought or emotion dominating it. If the emotion is weak and not vital, there is a shorter line of action.

In making a cross, start with the upstage foot and, other things being equal, walk in front of the other character. (Only rarely will necessity of conditions demand that the cross be made behind.) This is because the moving figure catches the eye, and, since he is dramatically dominant, there should be no break in audience attention. The rule of social usage which says that it is discourteous to pass between people does not apply here as the actor-audience relationship is of another kind. So, while points of etiquette should be regarded within the scene itself in the inter-character business, the whole must be kept pictorially and dramatically effective for the audience.

At the conclusion of a cross, be sure not to block. Walk well past the adjacent character and be sure not to stop in front of any other character who is in an upstage position.

As a rule, cross only on your own line. In those rare occasions when you must do otherwise, be sure not to cross in front of another character when he is speaking.

When you go to a position on the stage, go with decision

CROSSES AND TURNS

and stay there until it is time for the next move. Don't fidget.

Go to some definite place,—a window, door, piece of furniture, a tree, log, etc. The term " cross to nowhere " was coined by one director to describe a cross which goes away from a scene with no apparent destination. It is meaningless and ineffectual.

A turn is usually made toward the audience, the actor's face thus kept in view. Sometimes, the effect is heightened by the reverse action; perhaps the character left standing with his back to the audience. This type of turn and position must be used with discretion, however, and a full understanding of theatric effectiveness. The type of costumes worn and both the preceding and subsequent stage business will influence the choice.

In making a turn, avoid the awkward movement of stepping one foot across the other. So adjust the body balance that the turn can easily be made by pivoting on the balls of the feet with a minimum of movement, the upstage foot free to take the next step.

Practise making crosses and turns in various stage positions until you can do them smoothly, gracefully, and so inconspicuously that the audience is never aware of how they are being done. Nothing so quickly shows up the inexperience of the amateur actor as hesitant crosses and awkward turns.

*THE CHERRY ORCHARD

BY ANTON CHEKOV

Translated from the Russian
by Hubert Butler

SCENE.—*A spacious room which is still called the nursery. A door* C. *opens on a rostrum with a banister and steps, with a door* R. *leading into* ANYA'S *room. The steps lead down to the nursery. Included in the furnishings are some pieces of children's furniture, toys, etc. There is also a door down* R.

CHARACTERS: MADAME RANEVSKY (*Lyubov Andreyevna*), *a landowner.*
ANYA, *her daughter, aged 17.*
VARYA, *her adopted daughter, aged 22.*
GAEV, LEONID ANDREYEVICH, *her brother.*
LOPAHIN, YERMOLAI ALEXEYVICH, *a merchant.*
SEMYONOV-PISHCHIK, *a landowner.*
DUNYASHA, *a maid.*
FIRS, *an old footman of 87.*
YASHA, *a young footman.*
CHARLOTTA, *a governess.*
EXTRAS.

(LOPAHIN *is discovered, reading, as* DUNYASHA *moves about, arranging flowers, furniture, etc. A door slams off and buzz of talk crescendo till general entrance.*)

LOPAHIN. (*Listening*) Listen! (*Rises.*) I think that's them coming.

* Copyright, 1934, by Hubert Butler

DUNYASHA. Yes, that's them! (*Runs to banister.*) What's come over me? I've got the shivers!

LOPAHIN. (*Going out* C.) Yes, there they are now. Come out and meet them. I wonder will she know me? It's five years since we've seen each other.

DUNYASHA. (*Leaning against banister, agitated*) Oh, I'm going to faint, I'm going to faint. [*Exit,* C.

(*The stage is empty while noises of arrival are heard off.* FIRS *enters* C., *hobbles quickly across, leaning on his stick and muttering to himself, and goes off* R. *The hubbub outside increases. A voice says, " Let's come this way." Enter* LYUBOV, ANYA, *and* CHARLOTTA, *all in travelling clothes,* VARYA, *in a coat with a kerchief on her head,* GAEV, PISHCHIK, LOPAHIN, DUNYASHA, YASHA *and other servants follow with luggage.*)

ANYA. (*Entering first*) Let's come this way. Do you remember what room this is, Mamma?

LYUBOV. (*Joyously through her tears*) The Nursery! (*On steps, then crosses* D. L. C.)

VARYA. (*Crossing* D. L. *with two bags*) Oh, but it's cold. My hands are like ice! (*To* LYUBOV.) You'll find your rooms exactly the same, Mamma, the White room and the Mauve room.

(CHARLOTTA, LOPAHIN *and* PISHCHIK *talk together audibly.*)

LYUBOV. (D. C. *holding* GAEV'S *arm: both back to audience*) The dear old nursery—what a sweet room it is. I used to sleep here when I was a child. (*Cries.*) And now I *feel* just like a child. (*She kisses her brother and* VARYA *and then her brother again.*) And Varya hasn't changed a bit . . . our little Nun!

(DUNYASHA *crosses to* LYUBOV *and takes off* LYUBOV'S *coat, during which* YASHA *crosses* C. *to* D. R., *carrying luggage.*)

GAEV. The train was two hours late. Did you ever?

The way they run things! (*Goes out* D. R. *arm-in-arm with* LYUBOV. *Servants follow with luggage, etc.*)

(*Only* ANYA *and* DUNYASHA *are left, the others having gone off* D. R.)

DUNYASHA. We've been waiting for you for ages. (*Takes off* ANYA'S *hat and coat.*)

ANYA. (*Crosses to banister*) I didn't sleep the whole four nights on the train, and now I'm simply perishing.

DUNYASHA. It was Lent when you went away . . . we were having snow and frost, and now look at it . . . ! (*Crosses to* ANYA *and embraces her.*) Oh, my dear! We thought you were never coming, sweetheart, darling!

ANYA. (*Glancing tenderly into the door of her room*) My room, my window! I don't feel as if I'd been away at all! I'm home! Tomorrow morning I'll get up and run into the garden. . . . Oh, but I'd give anything to get to sleep! I didn't close an eye the whole way. I was so worn out with all the fussing.

DUNYASHA. Pyotr Sergeyich arrived the day before yesterday.

ANYA. (*Delightedly*) Petya! (*Crosses quickly back to banister.*)

DUNYASHA. He's asleep in the bath house; he's got his bed and all there. "I'm afraid of being in their way," says he. (*Looking at her watch.*) I was to have woken him, but Varvara Mihailovna told me not to; she said, "Don't wake him whatever you do".

VARYA. (*Comes in* D. R. *with a bunch of keys on her belt*) The coffee, Dunyasha, and look sharp! Mamma's asking for coffee.

DUNYASHA. In two minutes . . .   [*Goes out* D. R.

VARYA. Well, thank goodness you've come. (*They sit on steps.*) You're home again. My pet lamb is home! My own pretty pet. (*Embraces her.*)

ANYA. Oh, what I've been through.

VARYA. I can just imagine.

ANYA. It was Holy Week when I left, frightfully cold—and Charlotta would talk the whole way. . . . What ever made you tie me to Charlotta's apron strings?

VARYA. Oh, you couldn't travel alone, dearest, at seventeen.

ANYA. It was cold and snowy when we got to Paris and my French is hopeless. Mamma lives on the fifth floor and I went up to her; there were a lot of French people there, some ladies and an old priest with a little book, and it all was so uncomfy and smelt of tobacco. I suddenly got so sorry for Mamma, I put my arms around her neck and hugged her. She was very sweet and began to cry . . .

VARYA. (*Through her tears*) Oh, don't go on! I know, I know.

ANYA. She's sold the villa at Mentone and she'd absolutely nothing left. I hadn't a farthing left either, we'd only just had enough for the journey. But Mamma simply doesn't understand; when we had meals in the station restaurants she always ordered the most expensive things and tipped the waiters a rouble each. And Charlotta's as bad. And Yasha has to have exactly the same as us; it's simply awful. You know Yasha's Mamma's valet now; he's come back with us.

VARYA. Yes, I've seen him, the scamp!

ANYA. Well, tell me—did you pay the interest that was owing?

VARYA. Where was the money to come from?

ANYA. Oh dear, oh dear!

VARYA. They're going to sell out the place in August.

ANYA. Oh, dear!

LOPAHIN. (*Pokes his head round door and moos like a cow*) Mooo! [*He vanishes.*

VARYA. (*Through her tears*) Oh, I could just . . . (*Rises and shakes her fist at the door.*)

ANYA. (*Rising and embracing* VARYA) Varya, has he asked you to marry him? (VARYA *shakes her head.*) I'm sure he is fond of you; why don't you fix it up between you? What's the good of waiting?

VARYA. There'll never be anything between us, if you ask me. . . . It makes me heart-sick even to see the man. God help him! (*In a different voice.*) You've got a new brooch like a bee!

ANYA. (*Miserably*) Mamma bought it.
[*She goes into her room.*
VARYA. (*Up on rostrum leaning on* ANYA'S *doorpost*) My pet's home again. My own pretty pet!

(*Scene may end here or continue as follows:*)

(DUNYASHA *enters with the coffeepot and starts making the coffee. Coffee things on table.*)

VARYA. (*As she stands near the door*) I dream about you all day long, my pet, all the time I am walking about doing the housekeeping. What a weight it would take off my mind if only we could find you a rich husband. I'd go off on my own into the wilderness and then to Kiev . . . and then to Moscow. I'd go from one holy place to another. I'd always be on the move. It would be heavenly.
ANYA. (*Off*) The birds are singing in the garden. What time is it?
VARYA. It must be quite three. It's time you went to bed, darling. . . . It would be heavenly . . .
ANYA. (*Coming out of her room*) We ought to break it to Mamma that Petya's here.
VARYA. I told them not to wake him. (*Pause.*)

(ANYA *sits on banister.* VARYA *takes hair brush from her and brushes* ANYA'S *hair, singing softly.* ANYA'S *speech should be broken with long pauses,* VARYA *singing quietly all the time.*)

ANYA. (*Pensively*) It's six years since father died. Then a month later my brother was drowned in the river, dear little Grisha, only seven and such a love. It was a terrible shock for Mamma and she went right away, away from everything; she turned her back on it all. (*Shudders.*) If she only knew how well I understand her. . . . Petya was Grisha's tutor—he might remind her.

(FIRS *comes in* D. R. *He has on a jacket and white waistcoat. Goes anxiously to coffeepot.*)

Firs. The mistress will take her coffee here. (*Puts on white gloves.*) Is it ready? (*Sternly, to* Dunyasha.) Come, girl! Where's the cream?

Dunyasha. Oh! Save us! [*Goes out quickly* D. R.

Firs. (*Fussing around coffee table*) Useless bag of tricks! (*Mutters.*) Back from Paris . . . the old master used to go to Paris, too . . . it was horses then . . . (*He laughs.*)

Varya. What's the matter, Firs? (*Crosses to him.*)

Firs. Yes, ma'am? (*Joyfully.*) The mistress is back. I've lived to see it . . . even if I die today . . .

(Lyubov *enters and crosses* D. C., Gaev *behind her.* Lopahin *and* Pishchik *heard off.* Lopahin *enters, crosses up* C. Pishchik *enters, crosses above sofa to* D. L. *and sits on armchair.* Gaev *moves* C. *to* Lyubov, *both facing upstage.*)

Gaev. (*During this speech* Lopahin *goes toward* Varya, *up* L.) Once upon a time you and I used to sleep in this room, sister dear. And now, strange to relate, I'm fifty-one.

Lopahin. Yes, time flies.

Gaev. *What* flies?

Lopahin. Time, I said, flies.

(Gaev *sits* D. R. C., Lyubov *sits on sofa,* Anya *goes to* Lyubov *from top of steps.* Lopahin *brings chair down and sits.*)

Anya. I'm going to bed. Sleep well, Mamma. (*Kisses her.*)

Lyubov. My own precious! Aren't you glad to be home! I simply can't realize it.

(Anya *says good-night all around, last to* Gaev, *and exits between* Gaev *and* Lopahin. Firs *gives coffee to* Lyubov *and* Pishchik. Lopahin *rises, gets his own, and comes down.* Firs *gets coffee and brings it to* Gaev *after* Anya *has left him.*)

ANYA. Good-night, Uncle.

GAEV. (*Kissing her face and hands*) God bless you! How like your mother you are! (*To his sister.*) You were exactly like that at her age, Lyubov.

[ANYA *goes to her room, yawning.*

LYUBOV. She's utterly worn out.

PISHCHIK. Oh, she's had a long journey.

VARYA. (*Coming between* LYUBOV *and* LOPAHIN,— FIRS, R. *of table, getting cushion from under table*) Well, gentlemen! It's three o'clock and time to say good-bye.

LYUBOV. (*Laughing*) You haven't changed a bit, Varya. Look, I'll just drink up my coffee and then we'll *all* be off! (FIRS *puts cushion under her feet.*) Thank you, Firs dear. I simply can't do without my coffee. I drink it day and night. Thank you, dear old fellow!

VARYA. (*Has got to* R. *of* LOPAHIN. *She starts to speak. He turns to look at her but she gets self-conscious and exits* D. R. *speaking*) Well, I'll just take a look whether they've brought all your things in.

LYUBOV. Is it really me sitting here? (*Laughs.*) I want to jump about and wave my arms. (*Hides her face in her hands.*) I'm so sleepy, too. I do love my country, I do love it. I couldn't look out of the carriage window. I cried the whole way. But coffee's got to be drunk all the same. Thanks, Firs, thank you, dear old fellow. I'm so glad you're still alive.

FIRS. The day before yesterday.

GAEV. He's got very deaf.

(FIRS *up to back of room.*)

LOPAHIN. I'll soon have to be leaving for Harkov—at five o'clock; isn't it a nuisance? I wanted to see something of you and have a chat. You're as wonderful as ever.

PISHCHIK. (*Breathing heavily*) More so, if you ask me. Paris fashions, too. . . . I'm completely bowled over.

LOPAHIN. Your brother here is always saying what a cad and an upstart I am, but what do I care? Let him say what he likes. (GAEV *rises* R., *to end of* R. *banister.*)

All I mind about is that you should trust me as you once did. . . . If only you'd look at me with those wonderful gentle eyes, as you used to! God forgive me—my father was a serf of your father and your grandfather before him, but you yourself, you did such a lot for me once upon a time that I've forgotten everything and love you as if you were one of my own . . . more than if you were one of my own.

LYUBOV. I can't sit still, I simply can't. (*She walks about, looking at objects in the room, carrying her coffee cup.* LOPAHIN *follows her round.*) I shan't survive so much happiness. Laugh at me if you like—I know I'm silly. My own dear bookcase! My little table!

GAEV. Nurse died while you were away.

LYUBOV. Yes, God rest her soul! So you wrote.

GAEV. And Anstasia's dead and Squinty Peter's left me and taken a place in town with the police inspector.

PISHCHIK. My little girl, Dashenka . . . asked to be remembered.

LOPAHIN. (L. *behind sofa*) I've a piece of good news for you, to cheer you up. (*Looking at his watch.*) I must rush off though; there's barely time to talk of it. Well, I can say it in a couple of words. As you already know, your cherry orchard is being sold to pay your debts —the sale is fixed for the 22nd of August—but there's no need to get worried, my dear, you can sleep in peace, for I've found a way out. (LYUBOV *gets more coffee and sits.*) Now just listen to my plan, please. Your estate is only twenty versts from the town and the railway runs alongside it. Well, if you divide up the cherry orchard and the land along the river into building plots and let them out for bungalows (LYUBOV *and* GAEV *exchange looks of disgust*) they ought to bring you in an income of twenty-five thousand roubles a year at the very least.

GAEV. Sorry, but you're talking nonsense.

LYUBOV. I don't quite follow you, Yermolay Alexeyich.

LOPAHIN. (*During speech* FIRS *creeps forward to eavesdrop*) . . . It's a magnificent site and a fine deep river—only, of course, you must get the land cleared. (*Crosses to window below* FIRS.) I mean take away all the old buildings, and this house, too, which is tumbling in, in any case, and cut down the old cherry orchard.

(LYUBOV *rises.* GAEV *bangs cup in saucer.*)

LYUBOV. Cut down the . . . ? My dear man, I'm sorry, but you simply don't understand. Our cherry orchard is a long way the most remarkable and interesting thing in the whole province.

LOPAHIN. The only remarkable thing about your orchard is that it is very large. It has a good crop every other year, but there's no market and you can't get rid of it.

GAEV. There's a reference to the orchard in the Encyclopedia.

LOPAHIN. (*Looking at his watch*) If we can't make up our minds and come to some decision, then on the 22nd of August the cherry orchard and the whole property with it will be put up for auction. Now you decide. It's the only way out, I promise you. It's your very last chance.

LADY WINDERMERE'S FAN

(Scene 1)

BY OSCAR WILDE

SCENE.—*Morning-room of* LORD WINDERMERE'S *house. Doors* C. *and* R. *and window opening on terrace* L.

CHARACTERS: LADY WINDERMERE.
   DUCHESS OF BERWICK.
   LADY AGATHA.
   PARKER, *the butler.*

(*The material used in these scenes is excellent for illustration of the technical points in high comedy.* AGATHA, *the daughter of the* DUCHESS OF BERWICK, *says not one word throughout the play but "Yes, Mamma." She creates the impression, however, of being much less ingenuous than she appears.)*

(As the curtain rises LADY WINDERMERE *is at table* R. *arranging flowers.)*

PARKER. *(Entering at* C.) Is your ladyship at home this afternoon?

LADY WINDERMERE. Yes, who has called?

PARKER. The Duchess of Berwick and Lady Agatha Carlisle.

LADY WINDERMERE. *(Hesitates for a moment)* Show them up.

PARKER. Yes, my lady. *(Goes off* C. *There is a short pause, after which* PARKER *reappears and announces the callers.)* The Duchess of Berwick and Lady Agatha Carlisle. [*Exit,* C.

DUCHESS OF BERWICK. *(Coming down and shaking hands)* Dear Margaret, I am so pleased to see you. You remember Agatha, don't you? *(Crossing* L. C.) No, no tea, thank you, dear. *(Crossing and sits on sofa.)* We have just had tea at Lady Markby's. Such bad tea, too. It was quite undrinkable. I wasn't at all surprised. Her own son-in-law supplies it. Agatha is looking forward so much to your ball tonight, dear Margaret.

LADY WINDERMERE. *(Seated* L. C.) Oh, you mustn't think it is going to be a ball, Duchess. It is only a dance in honor of my birthday. A small and early.

DUCHESS OF BERWICK. But of course it's going to be select. We know that, dear Margaret, about your house. It is really one of the few houses in London where I can take Agatha. I don't know what Society is coming to. The most dreadful people seem to go everywhere. *(Rising and going to* C.) How sweet you're looking! Where do you get your gowns? *(Crosses to sofa and sits with* LADY WINDERMERE.) Agatha, darling!

AGATHA. Yes, Mamma. *(Rises.)*

DUCHESS OF BERWICK. Will you go and look over the photograph album that I see there?

AGATHA. Yes, Mamma. *(Goes to table* L.)

DUCHESS OF BERWICK. Dear girl! She is so fond of photographs of Switzerland. Such a pure taste, I think. (*Very confidentially.*) But I really am so sorry for you, Margaret.

LADY WINDERMERE. (*Smiling*) Why, Duchess?

DUCHESS OF BERWICK. Oh, on account of that horrid woman. She dresses so well, too, which makes it much worse, sets such a dreadful example.

LADY WINDERMERE. Whom are you talking about, Duchess?

DUCHESS OF BERWICK. About Mrs. Erlynne.

LADY WINDERMERE. Mrs. Erlynne? I never heard of her, Duchess. And what has she to do with me?

DUCHESS OF BERWICK. My poor child! Agatha, darling!

AGATHA. Yes, Mamma.

DUCHESS OF BERWICK. Will you go out on the terrace and look at the sunset?

AGATHA. Yes, Mamma.   [*Goes off* L.

DUCHESS OF BERWICK. Sweet girl! So devoted to sunsets! Shows such a refinement of feeling, does it not? After all, there is nothing like nature, is there?

LADY WINDERMERE'S FAN

(Scene 2)

BY OSCAR WILDE

SCENE.—*Drawing-room in* LORD WINDERMERE'S *house. Door* R. U. *opening into ballroom where band is playing. Door* L. *through which guests enter. Door* L. U. *opens on illuminated terrace.*

CHARACTERS: LADY WINDERMERE.
DUCHESS OF BERWICK.
AGATHA.
MR. HOPPER.
EXTRAS.

(*The curtain rises on the room crowded with guests.* LADY WINDERMERE *is receiving them.*)

DUCHESS OF BERWICK. (C.) Mr. Hopper is very late. You have kept those five dances for him, Agatha! (*Comes downstage.*)

AGATHA. Yes, Mamma.

DUCHESS OF BERWICK. (*Sitting on sofa*) The last *two* dances you must pass on the terrace with Mr. Hopper.

AGATHA. Yes, Mamma.

DUCHESS OF BERWICK. The air is so pleasant there.

AGATHA. Yes, Mamma.

MR. HOPPER. (*Enters* L.) How do you do, Lady Windermere? How do you do, Duchess? (*Bows to* LADY AGATHA.)

DUCHESS OF BERWICK. Dear Mr. Hopper, how nice of you to come early. We all know how you are run after in London. We wish there were more like you. Do you know, Mr. Hopper, dear Agatha and I are so much interested in Australia. It must be so pretty with all the dear little kangaroos flying about. Agatha has found it on the map. What a curious shape it is! However, it is a very young country, isn't it?

MR. HOPPER. Wasn't it made at the same time as the others, Duchess?

DUCHESS OF BERWICK. How clever you are, Mr. Hopper. Now I mustn't keep you.

MR. HOPPER. But I should like to dance with Lady Agatha.

DUCHESS OF BERWICK. Well, I *hope* she has a dance left. Have you got a dance left, Agatha?

AGATHA. Yes, Mamma.

DUCHESS OF BERWICK. The next one?

AGATHA. Yes, Mamma.

MR. HOPPER. May I have the pleasure?

(LADY AGATHA *bows.*)

DUCHESS OF BERWICK. Mind you take great care of my little chatterbox, Mr. Hopper. (LADY AGATHA *and* MR. HOPPER *pass into ballroom. Music off stage. As it stops, guests come on from ballroom.*) But where is Agatha? Oh, there she is. (LADY AGATHA *and* MR. HOPPER *enter from the terrace.*) Mr. Hopper, I am very angry with you. You have taken Agatha out on the terrace, and she is so delicate.

MR. HOPPER. Awfully sorry, Duchess. We went out for a moment and then got chatting together.

DUCHESS OF BERWICK. Ah, about dear Australia, I suppose?

MR. HOPPER. Yes.

DUCHESS OF BERWICK. Agatha, darling! (*Beckons her over.*)

AGATHA. Yes, Mamma!

DUCHESS OF BERWICK. (*Aside*) Did Mr. Hopper definitely ——

AGATHA. Yes, Mamma.

DUCHESS OF BERWICK. And what answer did you give him, dear child?

AGATHA. Yes, Mamma.

DUCHESS OF BERWICK. My dear one! You always say the right thing!

*THE PSYCHOLOGICAL MOMENT

A supposed episode in the life of Mme. Dubarry

BY PATRICIA MORBIO

SCENE.—*A boudoir. Door* U. L. *At back* C. *French windows open out on a little balcony.*

CHARACTERS: MADAME D'AUTREMONT.
JEANNE, *a milliner's apprentice.*

(MADAME D'AUTREMONT *is discovered seated before her dressing table. She is putting the last touches to her toilette, humming to herself as she does so. Sud-*

* Copyright, 1931, Walter H. Baker Company

denly she stops, runs quickly to the window and peers eagerly out. She turns back into the room, frowning with disappointment. A bell rings off stage.)

MADAME. Ah, perhaps that is my new bonnet. (*She hurries back to the dressing table and seats herself, humming very determinedly. Enter* JEANNE, *colorfully dressed and a bit impudent in manner. On her arm she carries a decorative hatbox, tied with cherry-colored ribbons.*) Ah, there you are, Jeanne. And you've brought my bonnet!

JEANNE. Yes, Madame, and it is mos' enchanting—a bit *jeune fille*, to be sure, but that is perhaps as Madame would desire it. (*Unties ribbons of box as she is speaking, and lifts out bonnet.*)

MADAME. Oh, it is ravishing. (*Clapping her hands.*) Such flowers, such ribbons. Put it on me, Jeanne.

(JEANNE *leisurely walks to dressing table, surveying room as she goes.*)

JEANNE. (*Adjusting bonnet on* MADAME) It goes like this—or if Madame feels perhaps a bit roguish—like this. (*Tilting it a little.*)

MADAME. (*Smiling at effect—then hastily returning to a more dignified manner*) The first way is more suitable, Jeanne.

JEANNE. (*Shrugging her shoulders*) As Madame wishes. (*Adjusts bonnet.*)

(*A long whistle is heard. Both stop and listen.*)

MADAME. (*Confusedly*) Why—er—er —— (JEANNE *starts toward window.* MADAME *speaks her name sharply.*) Jeanne!

JEANNE. (*Respectfully*) Yes, Madame. (*A pause while* MADAME *appears to be studying the effect of the bonnet.*) Madame is then pleased?

MADAME. (*Abstractedly*) Yes, Jeanne.

JEANNE. Then I may go?

MADAME. Oh, no, Jeanne, wait. Sit down a moment.

I wish to speak to you. (JEANNE *sits on sofa. The whistle is heard again.* JEANNE *looks with fresh curiosity toward the window.* MADAME *appears not to notice anything.*) Jeanne, what are your wages at Mme. Pressan's?

JEANNE. Five francs a week, Madame.

MADAME. If you will do a very slight service for me, I will give you twenty francs.

JEANNE. (*Crossing herself*) Oh, Madame, who do you want murdered?

MADAME. (*Laughing*) Not that, Jeanne, a much easier task, I assure you.

JEANNE. (*Craftily*) But, Madame, we are not allowed by Mme. Pressan to receive gifts or bribes ——

MADAME. (*Bristling with indignation*) Bribes? Who spoke of bribes? You are supposed to please the customers, are you not?

JEANNE. (*Sighing*) If it is possible, Madame.

MADAME. But this is very simple, and if you do it well and are discreet, I may give you twenty-five francs.

JEANNE. But Mme. Pressan said ——

MADAME. (*Impatiently*) Bother Mme. Pressan. (*Crosses to where* JEANNE *is sitting.* JEANNE *rises.*) Sit down, child. (*Puts cloak to one side and draws* JEANNE *down on sofa beside her.*) Now, Jeanne, you must listen to me. I am perhaps a little older and no doubt much wiser than you.

JEANNE. (*Meekly*) Yes, Madame.

MADAME. You must learn, my child, how to manage your own life. Of course you must do what your mistress tells you to, but in some of the outside matters, as it were, you must decide yourself what is best for you to do.

JEANNE. (*With a great show of innocence*) But le bon Dieu—He will take care of me if I am good.

MADAME. Of course, of course He will, but you are expected to think a little for yourself. Now (*producing some jingling coins from her bag*) when an opportunity like this comes to do a small service for a goodly sum, you should not hesitate. You must learn to recognize the psychological moment, my child, and then—(*the whistle again—more insistent than before.* MADAME, *with agita-*

tion, putting the coins into JEANNE'S *hand.*) Oh, you must do this for me ——

JEANNE. (*Looking at the money, but feigning indifference*) And what is it that Madame wishes me to do?

MADAME. Listen, my child. Below in the hedge, a friend of mine is waiting for certain information. It would be most indiscreet for Madame d'Autremont to be seen conversing from her balcony, perchance, but if little Mlle. Jeanne stands there, no one will notice.

JEANNE. (*Affronted*) Non?

MADAME. (*Smiling placatingly*) That is, no one of any importance. (JEANNE *sniffs, and tosses her head.*) You can carry my words to him, and his to me.

JEANNE. (*Brightening at the prospect of intrigue*) Oh, I see.

MADAME. (*Eagerly*) You will do it, then?

(JEANNE *hesitates—counts her coins again, bites her lips, nods dubiously at first, eyes downcast, then looks up at* MADAME *who takes out more coins and throws them into* JEANNE'S *lap who then continues to nod vigorously and joyously.*)

(*Scene may end here, or may continue as follows:*)

JEANNE. (*Jumping up, and stuffing the money into the pocket of her apron. Makes a curtsey*) It is a bargain, Madame. (*With a gesture toward the window.*)

MADAME. Good. Go to the balcony, singing " Sur le pont d'Avignon "—it is the signal.

JEANNE. (*Crosses to the window, stands leaning against the curtain and sings with elaborate carelessness*) Ah, M'sieu. I am the messenger for Madame. (*The following dialogue up to* JEANNE'S *last speech is conducted rather sotto voce.* JEANNE, *turning back to* MADAME.) Ah, Madame, he is there. Then what do I say?

MADAME. (*Fairly a-tremble, but wishing to be coy*) Tell him he comes late.

JEANNE. Madame says you come late. (*Then, after listening.*) He says, Madame, he has been waiting hours.

MADAME. Tell him that as usual he exaggerates.

JEANNE. Madame says that as usual you ex-ag-ger-ate. (*Laboring over the pronunciation. Listening again.*) He says it has seemed an eternity.

MADAME. Ask him if he is well and happy.

JEANNE. Are you well and happy? ... He answers not so much so as someone has the power to make him.

MADAME. (*Rising and crossing to dressing table*) Has he had tea?

JEANNE. Have you had tea? ... Not yet, Madame, as he is expecting a guest.

MADAME. Only one?

JEANNE. Only one? ... (*With difficulty.*) He says, Madame, only one—but that one is more than a legion of others.

MADAME. Is he quite sure she is coming?

JEANNE. Are you quite sure she is coming? What? You cannot hear me well? (*Moves to the other side of the balcony—still faces front.*) I said are you quite sure that she is coming? ... He says, Madame, that he can only hope she will not be so cruel as to deny him after all his waiting.

MADAME. Does he want her very much?

JEANNE. Do you want her very much? ... He says that Madame knows the answer to that question only too well. He asks will she cease to torture him, and come. ... Madame, excuse me. He is very handsome. I would not delay, if I were you.

MADAME. (*Haughtily*) You forget yourself, Jeanne. Even the confidential position in which I have placed you does not warrant such insolence. (*More gently.*) I'm sure you forget yourself.

JEANNE. (*Submissively*) Yes, Madame. Ah, Madame, M'sieu says he is dying of his impatience.

MADAME. (*Pleased and mollified*) Tell him it is good for the soul.

JEANNE. Madame says it is good for your soul. ... (*Horrified.*) He says he doesn't care about his soul—will Madame come to tea?

MADAME. That sounds a bit abrupt. Tell him I must yet think a bit.

JEANNE. Madame says she must think a bit. . . .
(*Smiling down upon him.*) He says will Madame please
cease to think ——
MADAME. And he is quite sure he is having only one
guest at tea?
JEANNE. And you're quite sure you are only having
one guest for tea? (*Coquettishly.*) He says, Madame,
that he is now not even sure of that one as she hesitates
so long.
MADAME. Foolish one. Remember, Jeanne, it is never
wise to condescend too quickly.
JEANNE. (*Demurely, with a side glance for the gallant
below*) Yes, Madame.
MADAME. Ask him if he is quite sure that his guest
will be very welcome?
JEANNE. (*Whose hand is quite evidently being held by
the gallant*) Are you quite sure that your guest will be
very welcome? . . . Yes, Madame, he says that now he
knows that his little guest will be most welcome.
MADAME. (*Thrilled visibly*) His little guest.—Then
—tell—him—tell him ——
JEANNE. Ah, Madame, whatever else I tell him will be
of my own making; for since you are so reluctant, he has
wearied of his pleading, and bids me to come instead.
You have given me such excellent advice, Madame, I
cannot help but take it. He is seizing my hand—and I,
Madame, I seize my psychological moment. Adieu. (*She
disappears behind the curtain of the balcony, laughing
lightly.*)

(MADAME *rushes to the window, sees that they are gone
and throws herself down in the chair before her
dressing table sobbing heart-brokenly, as the curtain
falls.*)

Copies of the complete plays from which these scenes
are made can be supplied by the publishers

Transitions

Transitions are moments of change. In characterization, they are moments of emotional change; in stage technique, they are moments during which the center of interest moves about.

Transitions occur (1) between scenes, (2) when the topic changes, and (3) when the relation between characters alters. In fact, whenever the dramatic situation changes, there should be a visual change in the stage picture. These shifts must be smooth, logical, and pictorially effective, always. Also, they must seem spontaneous, unstilted, and the audience never conscious of a previous adjustment.

Lacking the variety which transitions afford, a play seems to flatten out, to become static and monotonous; existing in sufficient numbers and well made, they give spirit and polish to a performance.

Experiment with the following scenes, trying to discover opportunities for transitions and see how perfectly you can make them.

*EETHER OR EYTHER

BY R. C. V. MEYERS

SCENE.—*A living-room.*

CHARACTERS: MRS. TURLINGTON.
MR. TURLINGTON.
TWITTER, *the maid.*
SIMPSON, *the butler.*

(*The* TURLINGTONS *are discovered in a charming domestic scene.* MR. TURLINGTON *is reading and* MRS. TURLINGTON *is doing needle point, or knitting.* TWITTER, *the maid, is arranging flowers at a side table.*)

MR. TURLINGTON. Listen to this charming bit.
MRS. TURLINGTON. (*Playfully pouting*) I wish I were as interesting as Ruskin.
MR. TURLINGTON. (*Throwing down book*) I'm a boor to allow Ruskin to claim a thought of mine while my wife is at my side! Ruskin is to blame for your displeasure!
MRS. TURLINGTON. Why, darling! I could never be displeased with you!
MR. TURLINGTON. You angel!
MRS. TURLINGTON. Twitter!
TWITTER. Ma'am?
MRS. TURLINGTON. Twitter, get married.
TWITTER. Which I will, ma'am, his name being Simpson, the butler, as asked me this very day.
MRS. TURLINGTON. You sensible thing! Twitter, you may have that blue silk of mine; I shall not want it any more.
TWITTER. Oh, thank you, ma'am! [*Exits.*

* Copyright, Walter H. Baker Company

Mrs. Turlington. What a happy omen! On the first anniversary of our marriage, our butler proposes to our maid!

Mr. Turlington. Charming, charming!

Mrs. Turlington. Edward, please go on with your Ruskin.

Mr. Turlington. While you are with me? Never.

Mrs. Turlington. I insist.

Mr. Turlington. You insist on my being rude?

Mrs. Turlington. Let's compromise . . . read aloud to me.

Mr. Turlington. I do so at your command. Otherwise ——

Mrs. Turlington. Read, or I shall think I have interrupted your pleasure.

Mr. Turlington. Anne, you are perfect. (*He kisses her hand, then opens book.*) Listen to this lovely bit, Anne.

Mrs. Turlington. Yes, dear.

Mr. Turlington. (*Reading*) "This is the true nature of home . . . it is the place of peace; the shelter not only from all injury, but from all terror, doubt and division. In so far as it is not this, it is not home."

Mrs. Turlington. Lovely, lovely; how like our own experience of the past year.

Mr. Turlington. Isn't it? (*Reading.*) "Wherever a true wife comes, this home is always round her . . ." No, that's not the place.

Mrs. Turlington. But it is lovely, all the same. And so true.

Mr. Turlington. Here is where I broke off. (*Reading.*) "The shelter not only from all injury, but from all terror, doubt and division. In so far as it is not this, it is not home; so far as the anxieties of the outer world penetrate into it, and the inconsistently-minded unknown, unloved and hostile world is allowed by eether husband or wife . . ."

Mrs. Turlington. (*Interrupting mildly*) Eyther.

Mr. Turlington. (*Laughingly*) "So far as the hostile society of the outer world is allowed by *eether* . . ."

Mrs. Turlington. (*Pausing in her work*) Eyther.

Mr. Turlington. (*Soberly and deliberately*) "Hostile society of the outer world is allowed by *eether* . . ."

Mrs. Turlington. I think you are wrong, dearest. It is *eyther!* So pronounced by most educated people.

Mr. Turlington. The authorities say . . .

Mrs. Turlington. Ah, but who are the authorities? I hope not the mere dictionary makers? Polite society is the best authority for the pronunciation of debatable words.

Mr. Turlington. But you said most educated people were the authorities.

Mrs. Turlington. The most educated people are not the most bookish, my dear. Education consists of . . .

Mr. Turlington. I may not be one of the most educated people, but I do say that EETHER . . .

Mrs. Turlington. Is incorrect.

Mr. Turlington. Anne, the origin of the word EETHER . . .

Mrs. Turlington. Pardon me, EYTHER.

Mr. Turlington. The origin of the word . . .

Mrs. Turlington. What are origins to me? You must confess that EYTHER is the more elegant pronunciation of the two.

Mr. Turlington. Elegance has nothing to do with the correct pronunciation of a word.

Mrs. Turlington. You probably mean that correctness has nothing to do with the elegance of a pronunciation. You are a trifle heated.

Mr. Turlington. (*Laughing in a forced manner*) I never was more cool in my life. Let us reason the thing out, my dear.

Mrs. Turlington. Certainly. But reasoning will never make me unreasonable. . . . I will never pronounce eyther, eether.

Mr. Turlington. Anne, do you mean to say that facts will not convince you?

Mrs. Turlington. Facts have nothing to do with the case. It is right or wrong, and in eyther event . . .

Mr. Turlington. Eether!

Mrs. Turlington. Eyther!

Mr. Turlington. Anne, do you wish to contradict me?

Mrs. Turlington. Contradict you? You are not responsible for the word, nor a dictionary.

Mr. Turlington. You insult me by insisting that I am neether . . .

Mrs. Turlington. Neyther.

Mr. Turlington. (*Loudly*) NEETHER elegant nor educated.

Mrs. Turlington. I merely said . . .

Mr. Turlington. I know what you said. And I say that the woman who will not be convinced by facts is a peculiar creature.

Mrs. Turlington. There may be a peculiar creature in the room, but it is not I. You may say EETHER to the end of the world, if you so wish! I know of no law to prevent you! But I must insist that I prefer EYTHER!

Mr. Turlington. It isn't what I wish, it is what is correct. Eether is, by admitted authorities, the correct pronunciation.

Mrs. Turlington. Your authorities, not mine.

Mr. Turlington. (*Rising*) Yours! A pack of affected society people.

Mrs. Turlington. (*Rising*) Yours! A tribe of hack-writers. And I will say . . .

(*Enter* Twitter *with flowers.*)

Twitter. Which Mrs. Turlington's mar and par has sent from the florist's, and smelling like perfumery they do, ma'am.

Mrs. Turlington. Twitter, come here!

Mr. Turlington. Come here, Twitter!

Twitter. Yes, ma'am. Yes, sir. Just as soon as I lay the flowers down.

Mr. Turlington. Never mind the flowers. Come here!

(Twitter *comes down front.*)

Mrs. Turlington. Twitter, I spoke to you first. You are not an educated person.

TWITTER. (*Nervously*) Which it isn't in the blood
. . . my mother never knowing her A B C's.
MRS. TURLINGTON. But I believe you possess common sense.
TWITTER. Which Mr. Simpson said when I said "yes" this morning, ma'am.
MRS. TURLINGTON. Twitter, do you say EETHER or EYTHER?
MR. TURLINGTON. Anne, what do you mean by this nonsense?
MRS. TURLINGTON. I wish to prove that my authorities are not all "affected society people." Twitter, is it EYTHER or EETHER?
TWITTER. (*Confusedly*) I never says neether.
MRS. TURLINGTON. Good! She never says neether, so she says NEYTHER.
MR. TURLINGTON. She means by her pronunciation that she would say EETHER when she uses the word.
MRS. TURLINGTON. She means . . .
MR. TURLINGTON. Twitter, what do you mean?
TWITTER. I don't know, sir. I mean, I don't know what you mean . . . which I am a bit confused.
MR. TURLINGTON. Answer me, Twitter. Is it EETHER that you mean?
MRS. TURLINGTON. It is EYTHER, is it not, Twitter?
TWITTER. (*Helplessly*) Ma'am?

(*Enter* SIMPSON *with flowers.*)

SIMPSON. The compliments of Mr. and Mrs. Turlington, Senior, the card says.
MR. TURLINGTON. Simpson!
SIMPSON. Sir?
MR. TURLINGTON. Come here, Simpson!
MRS. TURLINGTON. Edward, what is the meaning of this?
MR. TURLINGTON. Simpson, would you say EETHER or EYTHER?
SIMPSON. Sir?
MR. TURLINGTON. Don't be a fool, Simpson.
TWITTER. Oh, Mr. Simpson, which is which?

SIMPSON. Which is what? Twitter, have you been telling tales on me? Does it mean that, miss?

TWITTER. Me tell tales! Which it is not in the blood never to tell tales on nobody.

MRS. TURLINGTON. Simpson, my husband would ask you if you pronounce the word EYTHER, EETHER?

SIMPSON. Of course not, ma'am.

MRS. TURLINGTON. There, Mr. Turlington!

MR. TURLINGTON. Simpson, would you pronounce the word EETHER, EYTHER?

SIMPSON. I would not, sir. Twitter, you are in this.

MR. TURLINGTON. There, Anne!

MRS. TURLINGTON. Simpson, how *DO* you pronounce it?

SIMPSON. Pronounce what, ma'am? Twitter, did you say I did?

TWITTER. Did what?

MRS. TURLINGTON. This is delightful. Twitter, answer a question at once . . . is it EYTHER, or EETHER?

TWITTER. (*In tears*) It's Simpson, ma'am, and I wouldn't marry him if he hung with diamonds!

[*Dashes off wildly.*

SIMPSON. (*Throwing down flowers*) Cuss women!

[*Goes off with as much dignity as he can muster.*

MRS. TURLINGTON. Edward, this is simply outrageous! The vulgarity of the entire proceeding is beyond the power of endurance.

MR. TURLINGTON. You began it. I was reading to you a passage from Ruskin relative to the joys of a peaceful home, when you corrected me in the pronunciation of a word.

MRS. TURLINGTON. The word was EYTHER.

MR. TURLINGTON. The word was EETHER, I tell you, and EETHER it remains though the heavens fall!

MRS. TURLINGTON. (*Aghast*) You are positively terrible. It wouldn't surprise me if you resorted to violence. It is EYTHER, EYTHER, EYTHER! (*The last word is flung over her shoulder as she goes out.*)

MR. TURLINGTON. (*Striding up and down*) I never in my life saw anything so appalling as Anne's temper. And our first anniversary! And here we are expecting our parents to help us celebrate! (*Makes great effort to compose himself. Picks up book and is about to sit down. Hesitates. Looks in direction where* ANNE *disappeared. Throws down book in disgust and stalks off.*)

*THE LEAN YEARS

BY MARY KATHERINE REELY

SCENE.—*Interior of a small frontier shack. The board walls are unpapered. There is one window. The furnishings consist of one cookstove, newly blacked; one cupboard, made of two dry-goods boxes set one on top of the other—the shelves of same are covered with newspaper cut into crude scallops and fantastic patterns; one pine table, two pine kitchen chairs; one small cheap rocker.*

CHARACTERS: TOM CARSON.
LIZZIE CARSON, *his bride.*

(*Enter* TOM *and* LIZZIE CARSON. TOM *carries two old-fashioned travelling bags.* LIZZIE *precedes him into the room. Looks about her ecstatically.*)

LIZZIE. Oh, Tom! We're at home!
TOM. (*Dropping the bags and looking about him dubiously*) It's a poor home to bring you to, Lizzie.
LIZZIE. (*Examining everything*) Oh, the darling cookstove! Tom, I'll bet you blacked that up just for me! I know you never kept it so bright and shining while you were batching! (*Taking off lid and peeking in.*) And the fire all ready to light! Tom, bring a match and let's light it quick. The first fire in our own house!
TOM. Oh, come, Lizzie, take your coat off first. (*He helps her awkwardly to remove her coat [vintage of 1890] which has a very tight waist and very big sleeves. But before the queer little hat that perches so absurdly on her*

* Copyright, 1924, Walter H. Baker Company

head is removed, she spies the cupboard and darts over to that.)

LIZZIE. Oh, and the dish cupboard! You made it yourself! And the lovely shelf paper! Tom, don't tell me —— (*With a sparkle of a laugh.*) Don't tell me that you cut those yourself!

TOM. (*Proudly*) I did! Yes, sir; I did. Say, I tell you that I sat up nights working out that pattern. You know you fold it all up and then snip around with the shears—and till you open it out you don't know what you're going to get! I got some awfully queer-looking ones before I worked out this one. It don't look so bad, does it, Liz?

LIZZIE. Oh, Tommy! It's lovely—it's beautiful! (*With a little spring, she goes to his arms.*) Tom, I love everything in our home—because you made it, with your own hands,--for me.

TOM. (*His arms around her, one hand patting her shoulder*) It's a pretty poor home to bring you to, old girl. It's not much like what you been used to back in Ohio—only two little rooms—when you been used to a parlor and everything.

LIZZIE. But, Tom, this is *ours!* And I think we have lots of things—a cookstove, a cupboard, and dishes—and a table—and two chairs —— Oh, Tom, and that nice little rocker! Let me sit in it—I know you bought it for me. (*She breaks away to sit in the little rocker, rocking herself so hard that the absurd little hat that is still perched on her head wobbles dangerously.*)

TOM. (*Admiring her*) Lizzie, you'd look a lot more at home if you'd take your hat off.

LIZZIE. (*Laughing*) Oh, so I would. Help me to find the pins, Tom. (*Together they get the hat off.*)

TOM. Gosh, Lizzie, it looks good to see you here!

LIZZIE. It's good to be here, Tom—in our own home, on our own farm! Tom, isn't it wonderful to own a whole farm—all by ourselves!

TOM. Well, Lizzie, we don't exactly own it yet. There's that little matter of a mortgage to pay off.

LIZZIE. (*Snapping her fingers*) Pish! What's that! Why, we'll do that in no time, with good crops for a year or two. And in the meantime, think what fun we'll be having, living here all by ourselves. (*Jumping up.*) Now, tell me about the neighbors, Tom. Do we have any neighbors? (*Running to the window.*)

Tom. (*Following*) Well, you can't see from here, but we got neighbors all right. There's Shane's place only five miles down that way—nice folks they are—he's got a nice wife and two little boys. I'll take you over to see them some day, Lizzie. It's only five miles—that's nothing out here—we don't count distance like you do back east.

Lizzie. (*Bravely*) Five miles—why, that's nothing at all. We could drive over there in an hour most any day, couldn't we?

Tom. Well—our team could pretty near do it in an hour. And then about the same distance the other way there's some Swedes settled—they're nice folks, Lizzie, even if they don't talk much English. And work—say, a fellow has to hustle to keep up with them!

Lizzie. We'll keep up all right!

Tom. And awfully good-hearted folks—there's a Mrs. Nelson over there that's been sending me a batch of bread once in a while—say, she can cook!

Lizzie. Humph! Bet you've forgotten what good cooking is! But, Tom, it's time to get supper! Come on,—let's light our fire! The first fire in our own home! (*Seizing his hand and speaking more seriously.*) You do think we'll get on, don't you, Tom? That we'll pay off the mortgage—and everything'll be all right?

Tom. It's just got to be all right now you're here, Lizzie. Come on, now light your fire. (*He leads her to the stove, opens the door, and gives her a match.*) Here you are, Liz.

Lizzie. Tom, it will be an omen! Our first fire! If it burns well and the chimney draws, and it doesn't smoke— it will mean we are going to succeed!—Here—you light it!

Tom. No, I want you should, Lizzie. Our first fire!

(Lizzie *strikes the match, kneels slowly and reverently to apply it,* Tom *shielding her hands with his own.*)

THE WILD DUCK

BY HENRIK IBSEN

SCENE.—*Hjalmar Ekdal's studio living-room.*

CHARACTERS: GINA EKDAL, *Hjalmar's wife.*
HEDVIG, *her daughter, fourteen years old.*
HJALMAR EKDAL.

(GINA EKDAL *is sitting on a chair by the table, sewing.* HEDVIG *is sitting on the sofa, her hands shading her eyes, and her thumbs in her ears, reading a book.*)

GINA. (*Looks at her several times as if with suppressed anxiety; then she says*) Hedvig! (HEDVIG *does not hear her and* GINA *says in a louder tone.*) Hedvig!
HEDVIG. (*Moving her hands and looking up*) Yes, Mother.
GINA. Dear Hedvig, you mustn't sit there reading any longer.
HEDVIG. Oh, but my, Mother, mayn't I read a little longer? Just a little bit?
GINA. No, no; you must put the book away now. Your father doesn't like it. He never reads himself of an evening.
HEDVIG. (*Shutting the book*) No, father doesn't bother much about reading.
GINA. (*Putting down her work and taking up a pencil and small notebook from the table*) Can you remember how much the butter came to today?
HEDVIG. One krone and sixty-five ore.
GINA. That's right. (*Entering it.*) It's awful the amount of butter we get through here. And then there was the smoked sausage and cheese. Let me see—(*writing*)—and then there was the ham—h'm! (*Reckoning it up.*) Yes, it makes just ——
HEDVIG. And then there's the beer.

GINA. Yes, of course. (*Writing.*) It does run up—but it can't be helped.

HEDVIG. But then we didn't want a hot dinner, as father was out.

GINA. No, luckily. And then besides I took eight crowns, fifty ore for the photographs.

HEDVIG. Fancy! So much as that?

GINA. Exactly eight crowns, fifty ore.

(*A pause.* GINA *takes up her work.* HEDVIG *takes up paper and pencil and begins drawing something, shading her eyes with her left hand.*)

HEDVIG. Isn't it funny to think of father having a grand dinner at Mr. Werle's?

GINA. You can't say he's dining with Mr. Werle. You know it was his son who invited him.

HEDVIG. I'm looking forward so to father coming home. For he promised he'd ask Mrs. Sorby for something nice for me.

GINA. Yes, you may be sure there are plenty of good things in *that* house.

HEDVIG. (*Going on drawing*) And I'm just a little bit hungry, too. (*After a pause.*) Do you think they are still at table?

GINA. Goodness knows, but it's likely enough.

HEDVIG. Just fancy all the delicious things father'll have for dinner! I'm sure he'll be in good spirits and cheerful when he comes back. Don't you think he will, Mother?

GINA. Yes; but if we could only tell him we'd let the room.

HEDVIG. But there's no need to do that tonight.

GINA. Oh, it'll come in well enough, my dear. And it's no good to us.

HEDVIG. No, I mean we don't need it tonight, because father'll be in good spirits anyhow. We'd better save up the room for another time.

GINA. (*Looking across at her*) Are you glad to have something pleasant to tell father, when he comes home of an evening?

HEDVIG. Yes, for then he's much more cheerful.

GINA. (*Absently*) Oh, yes, there's something in that. (HJALMAR *enters* R. *and* GINA, *seeing him, throws down her work and gets up.*) Well, I never, Ekdal, you here already?

HEDVIG. (*Jumping up at the same time*) Fancy! You here so soon, Father?

HJALMAR. (*Putting down his hat*) Yes; most of them were leaving.

HEDVIG. So early?

HJALMAR. Yes, it was a dinner party. (*About to take off his top coat.*)

GINA. Let me help you.

HEDVIG. And me, too. (*They help him off with his coat and* GINA *hangs it up on the wall at back.*) Were there many people there, Father?

HJALMAR. Oh, no, not many. There were twelve or fourteen of us at table.

GINA. And I suppose you chatted with all of them?

HJALMAR. Oh, yes, a little.

HEDVIG. What sort of people were they?

HJALMAR. Oh, all sorts of people. There was Chamberlain Flor, and Chamberlain Balle, and Chamberlain Kasperson—and Chamberlain so-and-so—I don't know.

HEDVIG. Listen to that, Mother. He's been with nothing but Chamberlains.

GINA. Yes, they are awfully grand up at the house now.

HEDVIG. Did the Chamberlains sing, Father, or did they recite something?

HJALMAR. No, they only chatted. They wanted me to recite—but I wouldn't.

GINA. But surely you might have done that.

HJALMAR. No, one can't provide entertainment for everybody. (*Walking up and down impatiently.*) At any rate, I can't. I really don't see why I should provide entertainment, when I once in a way happen to go out. Let others do it. Here are these fine folk dining in grand houses day out, day in. Let them be thankful and amiable for all the good meals they get.

GINA. But surely you didn't say that!

HJALMAR. (*Humming*) Ah—h'm—h'm.

HEDVIG. (*Coaxingly*) How nice it is to see you in a dress coat. You look so well in a dress coat, Father.

HJALMAR. (*Posing*) Yes, don't you think so? And this one really sits faultlessly. It fits almost as if it had been made for me—a little tight in the armpits, perhaps. Help me, Hedvig. (*Takes off the coat.*) I'd rather put on my jacket. Where is my jacket, Gina?

GINA. Here it is. (*She fetches the jacket and helps him on with it.*)

HJALMAR. That's it. Be sure and remember to let Molvik have the dress coat the first thing in the morning.

GINA. (*Putting it down*) I'll see to it.

HJALMAR. (*Stretching himself*) Ah, after all, this is more comfortable. And, besides, this sort of loose, free, home dress, suits my whole style better. Don't you think so, Hedvig?

HEDVIG. Yes, Father.

HJALMAR. When I tie my necktie like this, with the loose ends, see, eh?

HEDVIG. Yes, that looks very well with the moustache and the thick curly hair.

HJALMAR. One can't call it exactly curly hair. I should rather say, wavy.

HEDVIG. Yes, for it's in such great curls.

HJALMAR. Waves!

HEDVIG. (*Pulling his jacket*) Father!

HJALMAR. Well, what is it?

HEDVIG. Oh, you know well enough what it is.

HJALMAR. No, I really don't.

HEDVIG. (*Laughing and pouting*) Oh, you do, Father. Now you mustn't tease me any more.

HJALMAR. But what is it?

HEDVIG. (*Shaking him*) Oh, nonsense. Now out with it, Father. You know all the good things you promised me.

HJALMAR. Ah! And to think I should have forgotten it!

HEDVIG. No, you only want to tease me, Father! Oh, it's too bad of you. Where've you put them?

HJALMAR. Well, I've not quite forgotten. But wait a

moment! I've got something else for you, Hedvig. (*Goes and searches in the pockets of his coat.*)

HEDVIG. (*Jumping and clapping her hands*) Oh, Mother, Mother!

GINA. You see, if you'll only wait ——

HJALMAR. (*With a paper*) See, here we have it.

HEDVIG. That? Why, that's only a piece of paper.

HJALMAR. That's the bill of fare; the whole bill of fare. Here is written " Menu "—that means bill of fare.

HEDVIG. Haven't you got anything else?

HJALMAR. I've forgotten the rest, I tell you. But you may take my word for it, these dainties are not very satisfying. Sit down there by the table and read out the list, and I'll describe the dishes to you. See here, Hedvig.

HEDVIG. (*Choking back her tears*) Thanks. (*She sits down, but does not read.*)

(GINA *makes signs to her;* HJALMAR *notices it.*)

HJALMAR. (*Walking up and down*) It is really most extraordinary what things the bread-winner of a family is expected to remember, and if he forgets the least of them—he's sure to be treated to black looks. Well, one gets used to that, too —— (*He continues to rant.*)

Copies of the complete plays from which these scenes are made can be supplied by the publishers

Motivation

There can be no stage business without a purpose and it must be motivated by the situation and character.

Avoid extraneous, superfluous business which has no meaning and only calls attention to itself. While it is necessary to have sufficient action to keep the play from being static, yet, unless there is a reason for every bit of this action, the result is merely nervous distraction wholly without dramatic value. An unmotivated act pulls away from the center of interest and takes a character out of the picture. Furthermore, the moment we become conscious of stage business as such, the dramatic force is lost.

Look through every speech for motivations that will be revealing, illuminating. Try to create *purpose,* then it will not be necessary to reduce the amount of movement. Action need not always be large, obvious movement, in order to be important and significant. Sometimes it is *re*action, " taking " a speech as well as giving it, or just observing and listening. These are often the hardest things to do, but if the company is not alive and interested, how can the audience be so?

It is said that, as a motion picture director, Boleslavsky was a master of mob scenes. With a comparatively few supers, he was able to produce the effect of a large crowd. His secret was to make every person a distinct character,—the coward, the bully, the sneak, the skeptic, the braggart, etc., each one reacting to the cues according to that character.

Whether movement is broad and sweeping, or quiet and subtle, be sure that it is set in motion by strong inner forces inherent in the character or the situation. The truer and deeper your understanding, the more capable will you be in discovering these forces.

*TRIFLES

by Susan Glaspell

SCENE.—*The kitchen in the now abandoned farmhouse of John Wright. A gloomy kitchen, and left without having been put in order,—unwashed pans by the sink, a loaf of bread outside the bread-box, a dish-towel on the kitchen table, and other signs of uncompleted work.*

Characters: MRS. HALE.
MRS. PETERS.

(Mrs. Peters, *the sheriff's wife, enters slowly. She is followed by* Mrs. Hale, *the wife of a neighboring farmer, who looks about fearfully as she enters. They listen to men's steps on the stairs, then look about the kitchen.*)

Mrs. Hale. I'd hate to have men coming into my kitchen, snooping around and criticizing. (*She arranges the pans by the sink.*)

Mrs. Peters. Of course it's no more than their duty.

Mrs. Hale. Duty's all right, but I guess that deputy sheriff that came over to make the fire might have got a little of this on. (*Gives the roller-towel a pull.*) Wish I'd thought of that sooner. Seems mean to talk about her for not having things slicked up when she had to come away in such a hurry.

Mrs. Peters. (*Who has gone to a small table in the* l. *rear corner of the room, and lifted one end of a towel that covers a pan*) She had bread set. (*She stands still.*)

Mrs. Hale. (*Eyes fixed on a loaf of bread beside the bread-box, which is on a low shelf at the other side of the room. Moves slowly toward it*) She was going to

* Copyright, 1924, Dodd, Mead and Company

put this in there. (*Picks up loaf, then abruptly drops it. In a manner of returning to familiar things.*) It's a shame about her fruit. I wonder if it's all gone. (*Gets up on the chair and looks.*) I think there's some here that's all right, Mrs. Peters. Yes,—here; (*holding it toward the window*) this is cherries, too. (*Looking again.*) I declare, I believe that's the only one. (*Gets down, jar in her hand. Goes to the sink and wipes it off on the outside.*) She'll feel awful bad after all her hard work in the hot weather. I remember the afternoon I put up my cherries last summer. (*She puts the jar on the big kitchen table, C. With a sigh she is about to sit down in the rocking chair. Before she is seated she realizes what chair it is; with a slow look at it, she steps back. The chair which she has touched rocks back and forth.*)

MRS. PETERS. Well, I must get those things from the front-room closet. (*She goes to the door at the right but, after looking into the other room, steps back.*) You coming with me, Mrs. Hale? You could help me carry them. (*They go into the other room; they reappear, MRS. PETERS carrying a dress and skirt, MRS. HALE following with a pair of shoes.*) My, it's cold in there. (*She puts the clothes on the big table and hurries to the stove.*)

MRS. HALE. (*Examining the skirt*) Wright was close. I think maybe that's why she kept so much to herself. She didn't even belong to the Ladies' Aid. I suppose she felt she couldn't do her part, and then you don't enjoy things when you feel shabby. She used to wear pretty clothes and be lively, when she was Minnie Foster, one of the town girls singing in the choir. But that—oh, that was thirty years ago. This all you was to take in?

MRS. PETERS. She said she wanted an apron. Funny thing to want, for there isn't much to get you dirty in jail, goodness knows. But I suppose just to make her feel more natural. She said they was in the top drawer in this cupboard. Yes, here. And then her little shawl that always hung behind the door. (*She opens stair door and looks.*) Yes, here it is. (*She quickly shuts door leading upstairs.*)

MRS. HALE. (*Abruptly moving toward her*) Mrs. Peters?

MRS. PETERS. Yes, Mrs. Hale?

MRS. HALE. Do you think she did it?

MRS. PETERS. (*In a frightened voice*) Oh, I don't know.

MRS. HALE. Well, I don't think she did. Asking for an apron and her little shawl. Worrying about her fruit.

MRS. PETERS. (*Starts to speak, glances up, where footsteps are heard in the room above. In a low voice*) Mr. Peters says it looks bad for her. . . . They say it was such a funny way to kill a man, rigging it all up like that.

MRS. HALE. That's just what Mr. Hale said. There was a gun in the house. He says that's what he can't understand.

MRS. PETERS. Mr. Henderson said coming out that what was needed for the case was a motive; something to show anger, or—sudden feeling.

MRS. HALE. (*Who is standing by the table*) Well, I don't see any signs of anger around here. (*She puts her hand on the dish-towel which lies on the table, stands looking down at table, one half of which is clean, the other half messy.*) It's wiped up to here. (*She makes a move as if to finish work, then turns and looks at loaf of bread outside the bread-box. She drops towel. In that voice of coming back to familiar things.*) Wonder how they are finding things upstairs. I hope she had it a little more red-up up there.

(*This scene may end here or continue as follows:*)

MRS. HALE. You know it seems kind of *sneaking*. Locking her up in town and then coming out here and trying to get her own house to turn against her!

MRS. PETERS. But, Mrs. Hale, the law is the law.

MRS. HALE. I s'pose 'tis. (*Unbuttoning her coat.*) Better loosen up your things, Mrs. Peters. You won't feel them when you go out.

(MRS. PETERS *takes off her fur tippet, goes to hang it on hook at back of room, stands looking at the under part of the small corner table.*)

Mrs. Peters. She was piecing a quilt. (*She brings the large sewing-basket, and they look at the bright pieces.*)

Mrs. Hale. It's log-cabin pattern. Pretty, isn't it? I wonder if she was going to quilt it or just knot it? (*She sits down at the big table, smoothing out a block with decision.* Mrs. Peters *pulls up a chair and joins* Mrs. Hale *at the table.* Mrs. Hale, *examining another block.*) Mrs. Peters, look at this one. Here, this is the one she was working on, and look at the sewing! All the rest of it has been so nice and even. And look at this! It's all over the place! Why, it looks as if she didn't know what she was about! (*After she has said this, they look at each other, then start to glance back at the door. After an instant,* Mrs. Hale *has pulled a knot and ripped the sewing.*)

Mrs. Peters. Oh, what are you doing, Mrs. Hale?

Mrs. Hale. (*Mildly*) Just pulling out a stitch or two that's not sewed very good. (*Threading a needle.*) Bad sewing always makes me fidgety.

Mrs. Peters. (*Nervously*) I don't think we ought to touch things.

Mrs. Hale. I'll just finish up this end. (*Suddenly stopping and leaning forward.*) Mrs. Peters?

Mrs. Peters. Yes, Mrs. Hale?

Mrs. Hale. What do you suppose she was so nervous about?

Mrs. Peters. Oh—I don't know. I don't know as she was nervous. I sometimes sew awful queer when I'm just tired. (Mrs. Hale *starts to say something, looks at* Mrs. Peters, *then goes on sewing.*) Well, I must get these things wrapped up. They may be through sooner than we think. I wonder where I can find a piece of paper and string.

Mrs. Hale. In that cupboard, maybe.

Mrs. Peters. (*Looking in cupboard*) Why, here's a bird-cage. (*She holds it up.*) Did she have a bird, Mrs. Hale?

Mrs. Hale. Why, I don't know whether she did or not—I've not been here for so long. Maybe she did.

Mrs. Peters. (*Glancing around*) Seems funny to

think of a bird here. But she must have had one, or why would she have a cage? I wonder what happened to it.

MRS. HALE. I suppose the cat got it.

MRS. PETERS. No, she didn't have a cat. (*Examining the cage.*) Why, look at this door. It's broke. One hinge is pulled apart.

MRS. HALE. (*Looking, too*) Looks as if someone must have been rough with it.

MRS. PETERS. Why, yes. (*She brings the cage forward and puts it on the table.*)

MRS. HALE. I wish if they're going to find any evidence they'd hurry up about it. I don't like this place.

MRS. PETERS. But I'm awful glad you came with me, Mrs. Hale. It would be lonesome for me sitting here alone.

MRS. HALE. It would, wouldn't it? (*Dropping her sewing.*) But I tell you what I do wish, Mrs. Peters. I wish I had come over sometimes when *she* was here. I—(*looking around the room*)—wish I had.

MRS. PETERS. But of course you were awful busy, Mrs. Hale—your house and your children.

MRS. HALE. I could've come. I stayed away because it weren't cheerful—and that's why I ought to have come. I—I've never liked this place. I dunno what it is, but it's a lonesome place and always was. I wish I had come over to see Minnie Foster sometimes. I can see her now —— (*Shakes her head.*)

MRS. PETERS. Well, you mustn't reproach yourself, Mrs. Hale. Somehow we just don't see how it is with other folks until—something comes up.

MRS. HALE. Not having children makes less work—but it makes a quiet house, and Wright out to work all day, and no company when he did come in. Did you know John Wright, Mrs. Peters?

MRS. PETERS. Not to *know* him; I've seen him in town. They say he was a good man.

MRS. HALE. Yes,—good; he didn't drink, and kept his word as well as most, I guess, and paid his debts. But he was a hard man, Mrs. Peters. Just to pass the time of day with him —— (*She shivers.*) Like a raw wind that gets to the bone. (*She pauses, her eyes falling on the cage.*) I should think she would have wanted a bird. But where do you suppose it went? (MRS. PETERS *shakes her head.*) You didn't know—her?

MRS. PETERS. No, I never saw her until yesterday.

MRS. HALE. She—come to think of it, she was kind of like a bird herself—real sweet and pretty, but kind of timid and—fluttery. How—she—did—change. (*Silence; then as if struck by a happy thought and relieved to get back to everyday things.*) I tell you what, Mrs. Peters, why don't you take the quilt in with you? It might take up her mind.

MRS. PETERS. Why, I think that's a real nice idea, Mrs. Hale. There couldn't possibly be any objection to it, could there? Now just what would I take? I wonder if her patches are in here—and her things.

(*They look in the sewing-basket.*)

MRS. HALE. Here's some red. I expect this has got sewing things in it. (*She brings out a fancy box.*) What a pretty box. Looks like something somebody would give you. Maybe her scissors are in here. (*She opens box. Suddenly puts her hand to her nose.*) Why—(MRS. PETERS *bends nearer, then turns her face away*)—there's something wrapped up in this piece of silk.

MRS. PETERS. Why, this isn't her scissors.

MRS. HALE. (*Lifting the silk*) Oh, Mrs. Peters—it's——

MRS. PETERS. (*Bending closer*) It's the bird.

MRS. HALE. (*Jumping up*) But, Mrs. Peters—look at it! Its neck! Look at its neck! It's all—other side to!

MRS. PETERS. Somebody wrung—its—neck!

(*Their eyes meet. A look of growing comprehension, of horror. Steps are heard outside.* MRS. HALE *slips box under quilt pieces, and sinks into her chair.* MRS. PETERS *sits down. The two women sit there, not looking at one another, but as if peering into something and at the same time holding back. When they talk now it is in the manner of feeling their way over strange ground, as if afraid of what they are saying, but as if they cannot help saying it.*)

MRS. HALE. She liked the bird. She was going to bury it in that pretty box. (*With a slow look around her.*) I wonder how it would seem never to have had any children around. (*Pause.*) No,—Wright wouldn't like the bird—a thing that sang. She used to sing. He killed that, too.

MRS. PETERS. (*Moving uneasily*) We don't know who killed the bird.

MRS. HALE. (*Meaningly*) I knew John Wright.

* A HEART TOO SOON MADE GLAD

BY WARREN BECK

SCENE.—*The reception room of a girls' dormitory in a mid-western college. The time is early evening.*

CHARACTERS: DICK ROBERTS.
GEORGE.
BOB.
LOUISE.
NORMA.

(*When the curtain rises,* DICK ROBERTS *is pacing the floor restlessly.* GEORGE *comes bustling in. He is conscientiously collegiate in clothes and manner, quite the opposite from* DICK, *who is studiously sophisticated.*)

GEORGE. Well, well, if it isn't Dick!
DICK. Hi, George. How's everything?
GEORGE. Great. I've got a wonderful date,—the keenest woman in college.

* Copyright, 1931, Walter H. Baker Company

DICK. That's hard to explain.
GEORGE. S'fact. They've just gone to coax the pretty creature down out of her room.
DICK. Coax? Don't worry; she'll come without coaxing. Not that I mean to flatter you, George; they always come.
GEORGE. You should have heard how I had to beg her for the date.
DICK. Yes, you would.
GEORGE. I don't know about that.
DICK. I simply meant that you would be foolish enough to beg for a date.
GEORGE. Well, I got the date, didn't I?
DICK. Yes, and how? The end doesn't justify the means.
GEORGE. It does this time. Wait until you see who she is.
DICK. Wake up, George. I know every girl on the campus, and they're not goddesses, they're just—female people.
GEORGE. Well, here you are, parked in the parlor. I guess you're not here to do your collateral reading.
DICK. I'm not dating, George. I'm here on business.
GEORGE. Yes?
DICK. Yes.
GEORGE. I may be dumb enough to coax the girls for dates, but I won't believe that.

(BOB *enters the room. He appears sturdy and sensible, well-dressed and genial. He has an easy manner and a complacent voice.*)

BOB. Hello, hello. Dick, what's the big idea? Didn't you tell us at dinner that you weren't dating?
DICK. I'm not.
GEORGE. He says he's here on business.
BOB. If you want to put it that way, so am I.
DICK. No, I mean I'm not dating—just calling.
GEORGE. That's a fine distinction.
DICK. It's a distinction, just the same.
BOB. Where is the difference, Dick—in the price?

Dick. No, in the motive. You date for pleasure; you call because of a sense of duty.

George. Sense of duty? Didn't know you had one.

Dick. I'm usually able to keep it pretty well under control, George.

Bob. Well, even a call made because of a sense of duty will be something for the poor child. A bright memory to cherish—a burning entry for her diary.

George. I wonder how many snappy diary lines Dick has inspired.

Dick. Don't be foolish. The girls I date don't have time to keep diaries.

Bob. Say, has either one of you seen this new girl? Just entered school? What's her name . . . ?

George. Gloria Ferguson?

Bob. That's it.

George. I've seen her at a distance.

Bob. Have you seen her, Dick?

Dick. Hadn't even heard of such a person.

George. You will.

Dick. Yes?

Bob. They say she's a beauty.

George. She is. She's a blonde.

Dick. What? Another blonde! I'd like to see something new—for instance, a girl with violet hair and yellow eyes, dead white skin and blue lips. But there's no variety.

George. I'm strong for blondes, myself.

Dick. Well, don't say anything about it. The blonde has already had too much encouragement.

Bob. Whatever this Gloria Ferguson is, they say she's the last word.

Dick. The ultimate utterance, huh? There isn't such a thing.

George. She's slim and snappy looking. I'll bet she can dance.

Dick. Oh, all of them can dance, more or less. All of them have about the same bag of tricks. You've heard of the Alger books—that's the way it is with girls. Same old story every time, with just a change in names.

George. Well, girls are only human, after all. You said so yourself.

DICK. Human? That's just what they aren't.
BOB. What's the matter? Has somebody been letting you break your heart again?
DICK. Not at all. I'm not airing a grievance; I'm talking sound theory.
GEORGE. What's wrong with the girls? What do you expect of them?
DICK. I expect imagination and some feeling that isn't second-hand and calculated, and some disinterested, spontaneous action. I expect enough sense of dramatic propriety to avoid anticlimaxes. I expect that companionship shall be thought of as an art, in terms of symmetrical beauty, and not as a business, in terms of expediency.
BOB. Sounds like an ultimatum.
DICK. It is, as far as I'm concerned.
BOB. You expect too much.
DICK. Maybe so.
GEORGE. Better check up on this new woman. She might be the answer to your prayer.
DICK. Who, the blonde? Huh! One more slightly pretty girl, with an exaggerated notion of her own charms, and a morbid craving for constant attention.

(LOUISE *enters coyly. She is the fluttery type.*)

LOUISE. Good-evening.

(*The boys rise.*)

GEORGE. Hello, Louise. My, you look wonderful.
LOUISE. Oh, thanks. (*She makes a sentence of it.*)
GEORGE. We'd better run along if we want to see the second show.
LOUISE. Oh, are we going to the show? That will be . . .
GEORGE. Yes, they say it's fairly good.
LOUISE. I'm sorry I was so slow, but I . . .
GEORGE. That's all right. I didn't mind waiting.
LOUISE. That's so sweet of you.
GEORGE. So long, boys. [*They go out.*
BOB. He didn't mind waiting! Oi! Oi!

Dick. And he tells me he begged for that date!

Bob. Louise *is* a nut, isn't she?

Dick. The breathless baby type; says nothing at all so significantly. That's the kind I hate worst of all.

Bob. It's the kind a lot of fellows fall for.

Dick. Fellows like George, yes.

Bob. Almost anyone might—there's something about them.

Dick. It takes more than a breathless baby to get around some of us.

Bob. Some of *us?* You, for instance, I suppose—and the other two wise men.

Dick. Why, yes. Girls like that lack the one quality which I demand in a woman—and that's reality.

Bob. Nice, broad word—could cover a multitude of types. Makes it easy, Dick; you can crash for any type—a breathless baby, even—and then explain that she has reality.

Dick. Say, you'll never see me crash for a gasping blonde.

Bob. Well, take your choice. I suppose, then, it will be one of these snaky brunettes.

Dick. No. I'm off women from now on, Bob.

Bob. What, again?

Dick. I'm serious, Bob. I'm through with the whole sex.

Bob. Interesting!

Dick. You'll see.

Bob. Yes—and believe afterwards.

Dick. That's what I'm here for tonight. I'm going to break off with Norma.

Bob. Now what's the matter with Norma?

Dick. She's like all the rest—thinks I'm hers to keep.

Bob. I hope you know what you're doing. Norma's a good kid.

Dick. She *is* a good kid. I suppose it isn't altogether her fault.

Bob. No?

Dick. You see, Bob, it's this way. There are three girls ——

Bob. Oho! Aha!

Dick. They've all taken me too seriously.

Bob. The brazen, forward creatures!

Dick. Oh, I suppose I'm partly responsible for that. Well, things just got tighter and tighter, until I decided that the only fair way to do was to give up all three.

Bob. Big-hearted and impartial, aren't you?

Dick. Two of them live in my home town—I wrote to them. Now I'm going to tell Norma. Then I'll be free, and I'm going to stay that way.

Bob. How did you ever get in so deep? Did they lead you on?

Dick. Did you ever see a woman who wouldn't?

Bob. Sometimes they do their share.

Dick. Oh, I'm not denying I had my share in it too.

Bob. I know you did.

Dick. It seems to me, though, that I get more than my share of trouble. I seem to pick the stickers. I'm always getting tangled up.

Bob. Don't you realize by this time how it happens?

Dick. I suppose it's chiefly hard luck.

Bob. No, it's not luck nor chance; it's cause and effect.

Dick. You think you know all about it?

Bob. I know that I know. I've been watching you for quite a while. It's your awful fluency that does it.

Dick. I talk too much?

Bob. Yes, and too enthusiastically, and too well. See what I mean?

Dick. Yes. Perhaps you're right. But I get a big kick out of it, Bob. I think of crazy things to say, and I can't resist spinning them out.

Bob. Yes, and then the girls, just to make life more interesting, pretend to believe them.

Dick. They surely do.

Bob. And there you are—all fixed.

Dick. Yes. On Friday morning they expect you to go right on from where you left off Thursday night. They act as though a fellow's mood should never change.

Bob. Well, Dick, you should live and learn. If you're not careful you'll talk yourself into something one of these days.

Dick. It is fun to hand them a line, though.

Bob. There's only one remedy for your disease—sublimation.

Dick. Huh?

Bob. Psychological sublimation. You turn a tendency into other channels; you find new and comparatively harmless expressions for a troublesome impulse. For instance, you could sublimate your ardent conversational desires by writing poetry, or going in for public speaking, or even doing some house-to-house canvassing.

Dick. That might work—but would it be as much fun?

Bob. Probably not, but it wouldn't be as hazardous, either.

(Norma *enters. She is a charming girl, well-poised and mannered. The boys rise.*)

Norma. Hello, men.

Dick. Hello, Norma.

Bob. Hi, Norma.

Norma. Bob, Helen is looking around the hall for you.

Bob. (*As he moves toward door*) Does she think I'd stand in the hall all this time?

Norma. I don't know.

Dick. There you are, Bob. Now you'll have to square yourself for sitting down while you waited.

Bob. (*As he goes out*) Don't forget the serious purpose, Dick.

*THE MAID OF DOMRÉMY

by Joe Corrie

SCENE.—*A simply furnished living-room in the home of a peasant farmer in Lorraine, France, in the year 1429.*

Characters: JEANNE D'ARC.
PIERRE D'ARC, *her brother.*

* Copyright, 1935, by Joe Corrie

(JEANNE D'ARC, *a strongly built girl of about seventeen, sits rocking a cradle and singing a little folk-song as she rocks. Her brother,* PIERRE, *enters. He is the opposite of* JEANNE *in every way, slightly round-shouldered, and he walks in an attitude of fear. He looks at* JEANNE *for a moment or two, as if he were afraid to speak to her.*)

JEANNE. (*Looking up at him*) What is it, Pierre?

PIERRE. (*After a pause, and approaching nearer to her*) Jeanne, I'll rock the baby if you'll go and milk Praline.

JEANNE. Why should *I* milk Praline, Pierre? That is *your* task.

PIERRE. (*After a little shiver*) She kicks! I am afraid of her.

JEANNE. (*Not bitterly*) Afraid of her? You, a man grown, afraid of a cow because she kicks? What *is* going to happen to you, brother Pierre? (*He turns his face away from her.*) You're afraid to milk Praline. You're afraid to ride on the donkey. You're afraid to cross the river at the stepping-stones. You're afraid to shout names to the Burgundians of Maxey. You're afraid to join the Domrémy boys when they go fighting the Maxey boys over the river. . . . You hide when you see an English soldier coming. You're ready to cry when father speaks sharply to you, and you cannot sleep when mother speaks angrily. You're afraid of every little thing, Pierre.

PIERRE. (*Without turning; piteously*) I know! I know! But I cannot help it. (*Turning.*) I'm just as God made me.

JEANNE. (*Sadly*) I have had to shelter you ever since I can remember, Pierre.

PIERRE. God made you without fear.

JEANNE. God made me no better than any other girl. It is doing *your* work that has made me strong. Why don't you try hard to be a man, Pierre? You are a year older than me, you know, and yet you look just like a boy.

PIERRE. (*Pleading*) Go and milk Praline, Jeanne. If father knows she hasn't been milked yet, he will be angry with me.

JEANNE. (*Considers for a moment*) No, I *won't* milk her. I am only encouraging you and making you worse. (*She sings again to the child.*)

(PIERRE *is in a miserable state, and glances furtively toward the door.*)

PIERRE. But she'll kick! She'll spill the milk! She may kick me and *kill* me! Jeanne, I can't!

JEANNE. Pierre, you make me feel angry with you at times. Always that whimper and these tears. Why don't you make up your mind to fight your fears? Other boys are bold enough. Why aren't you?

PIERRE. I was just born as I am, and will never be anything else.

JEANNE. (*She rises and holds his hands in hers*) You could be, Pierre, if you tried hard enough.

PIERRE. I'm not strong. I'm ill.

JEANNE. Your body isn't strong because your mind is weak. If you were to say, "I *will* milk Praline!" and did it once—just once, Pierre, you would be a different boy. (*She squeezes his hands in her effort to arouse him.*)

PIERRE. Jeanne, you are hurting my hands!

(*She lets go her hold.*)

JEANNE. Pierre, you are hopeless. (*She looks so strong now, standing at her full height, compared with* PIERRE, *who is limp, with his head hanging.*) You should have been me and I should have been you. But I do the boy's work and you do the girl's. You sit and rock the cradle while I go and milk the cow that kicks. You clean the shoes while I go into Domrémy on the donkey. You make the beds while I kill the cockerel for Sunday's dinner. You shelter behind a hedge while I bring the swine in from the field. Even when I was much smaller than you and we used to fight the Maxey children, you used to hide while we stoned them and chased them. Then you say I am strong. I have had to be, Pierre, to make up for your weakness.

THE MAID OF DOMRÉMY

PIERRE. No, no! You were born strong by God, and I was born weak.

JEANNE. Do not blame God, Pierre! Put your trust in Him, and you will grow stronger.

PIERRE. I *have* tried to put my trust in God, Jeanne. I have prayed and prayed, but He never hears me.

JEANNE. Because you have no faith. You cannot fool God, brother. Give yourself wholly to Him, and He will send His saints to help you.

PIERRE. God only sends His saints to girls. I don't think He loves boys.

JEANNE. (*Sadly*) Always excuses. Always blaming someone else, never yourself. Oh, Pierre! And France needs men that are strong and brave. France will never have peace till the English are driven away. And when will that ever be if you are the kind of boy she is depending on?

PIERRE. The English will never be driven from France. It is God's will that they are here.

JEANNE. Has God not given them a country of their own?

PIERRE. Go and milk the cow, Jeanne.

JEANNE. And wouldn't you like to chase them back to their own country some day?

PIERRE. God has said that He will send a saint one day to send them home.

JEANNE. You have heard father tell that story so often, Pierre. But you know she may not come yet for years.

PIERRE. Father says it will come to pass some day soon. Go and milk the cow, Jeanne.

JEANNE. Very well, I'll do it once more. But you will try it yourself tomorrow, won't you?

PIERRE. Yes, yes!

JEANNE. You will pray hard tonight?

PIERRE. Yes! Hurry, Jeanne, before father comes home.

JEANNE. Rock the cradle, then.

(*He goes gladly to the cradle and begins rocking it.* JEANNE *looks down on him.*)

PIERRE. (*Looking up ashamedly*) If I had voices speaking to *me* I would ——

JEANNE. (*Interrupting him angrily*) Do not speak about my voices! *You* do not understand. (*He hangs his head.* JEANNE, *dreamily.*) My voices! Ah! . . .
[*She goes outside proudly and gladly.*

(PIERRE *watches her go with a bit of a sneer on his lips.*)

Copies of the complete plays from which these scenes are made can be supplied by the publishers

Stage Business

Who thinks up all the action in a play? The director, chiefly. Most playwrights merely suggest stage business in a very general way. It is the director's imagination which makes the play come to life, creating at the time a harmonious blend with his cast and stage. The good actor understands what is needed and does his part.

Have you had the experience of reading a play, then seeing it performed by a fine company? Did you find yourself asking, " Where did it say to do all that?" Can you answer your own question now?

Ability to invent interesting and illuminating stage business grows with experience, but here are a few guides.

1. Business *which must be there,* usually revealed in the lines themselves, as, " I will go now,"—" Here is the book you asked for," etc.

2. Business for *delineation of character,* as peering over the top of eyeglasses, chuckling, knitting, etc. A good character portrayal is made up of minute details but must not be overworked.

3. Business to *reveal state of mind.* Examples: twisting corner of apron, biting the lips, tapping with pencil, powdering the nose. This type of business must be consistent with the character, used with discretion and restraint. It will usually occur during moments of transition.

4. Background business for *atmosphere, local color, or mood,* as dancing, tea drinking, an office worker at a desk, setting the table, or ironing.

5. Business for *pointing and emphasis.* This may be any one of a countless variety of movements which serve to reinforce the effect of the uttered thought. Even such simple acts as sitting or rising can be done at such a time and in such a way as to emphasize a word or two, making that particular thought stand out more vividly.

In the following scenes, exert your imagination and ingenuity to find opportunities for as many kinds of business as possible. Remember, though: *All action must be motivated.* Everything done must have an apparent reason.

*THE KELLY KID

BY KATHLEEN NORRIS AND DAN TOTHEROH

SCENE.—*The kitchen of the Murphy family on a hot June afternoon. It is a dark, smoke-stained kitchen with a door, back* C., *opening on the back porch.* L. *and* R. *of the back door are windows. A table, down* L., *has tea things on it. A door,* R., *leads into a bedroom. Three chairs are drawn up to the table. Above the table an ironing-board is stretched across the backs of two chairs.*

CHARACTERS: MRS. CAHILL.
MRS. MURPHY.
MRS. CALLAHAN.
ELLEN MURPHY.
ROBBIE KELLY.

(*When the curtain rises,* ELLEN MURPHY, *the 20-year-old daughter of* MRS. MURPHY, *is ironing, using an old-fashioned iron. About the table, seated and having tea, are the little widow* CAHILL, MRS. CALLAHAN *and* MRS. MURPHY. *They are discussing a very vital subject, and they lean toward each other, their keen eyes sparkling. Just now they have all raised their teacups and have all taken a deep drink, and now they put their cups down in their saucers and begin again.*)

MRS. MURPHY. (*The pessimist*) There's no good in that Kelly Kid, I've always said it!

MRS. CAHILL. (*Bitterly*) Glory be to the everlasting glory of God, but some harm will come to that child if they don't lock him up safe in jail!

* Copyright, 1926, Kathleen Norris

Mrs. Murphy. (*Darkly*) They'll get 'um yet!

Ellen. (*Laughing as she irons*) You're a grand lot of glooms! I wonder you wouldn't sit in the hot kitchen, a day like this! Why don't you go out in the back yard with grandpa and sit under the trees?

Mrs. Cahill. (*Dismally*) These are bad days out-o'-dures, wid all the flu that's in it.

Mrs. Murphy. That's right, Mrs. Cahill, dear. That's perfectly right. The fresh air's full of it.

(*The three women nod and drink their tea again, and again put down their cups all together.* Ellen *smiles at them and hums softly as she works.*)

Mrs. Cahill. (*With a sigh and another shake of her head*) It's boys like him what grows up to fill the jails and rob the poor boxes.

Mrs. Callahan. (*Thoughtfully. She is the level-headed member of the trio*) I don't know is he bad, or is he just wild and free with the bold spirits that's in him. . . . I seen 'um yesterday and I tuk it upon myself to stop 'um and give 'um a word. "Robert," I says to 'um, "yure good mother that's dead would turn in her grave if she could see the way you'll be carrying-on," I says. He gives me a bold, ugly look out of his bold face —— (*Her voice drifts away into silence.*)

Mrs. Murphy. (*With feeling*) Oh, he's a bad one! But this new cop on the beat, Hamilton, will get 'um! Ould Falley would never touch wan of thim boys, and they streelin' all over the place like Ayrabs! But this feller's a mean sort of weasel, and he'll get 'um.

Mrs. Cahill. Indeed and he will! He got Jawnny Fay last week and Big Jawnny give 'um such a lickin' when he heard that he'd been took to the Juvenile, that Rosy Fay come runnin' over, the way she wouldn't hear the child holler.

Ellen. (*With warmth*) Yes, and I think it was a dirty shame to arrest young Johnny! It's the Kelly Kid that's the ringleader, and he always goes scot-free. When Falley was on the beat, of course the whole pack knew they were safe, but this *Hamilton* is another pair of shoes ——

Mrs. Cahill. I don't know where ever a *cop* would get a name like *Hamilton*.

Mrs. Callahan. He's none of our sort. He's a hard, mean kind of man, and God help Robbie Kelly the day he lays hands on 'um.

Mrs. Cahill. Well, Robbie has a very ugly stepmother—she's a nosey, wild sort, Daze.

(*The other women nod and sip their tea.*)

Mrs. Murphy. (*Sighing*) He had a good mother.

Mrs. Cahill. Yes. And she had him in Sunday school, and she dressed him very nice, until the Sunday she was took, God rest her.

Mrs. Callahan. Yes. And Mack Kelly wouldn't have been a bad father to 'um if he'd lived. But Daze has got that young boy of her own that's never been right since he had scarlet fever, and him teethin', and she's hard on Robbie.

(*The other three nod again.*)

Mrs. Murphy. Sister Felix says that the child has a good heart in him, but he's wild. And he'll end in jail, and I'd never raise hand nor foot to keep him out of it! (*Her mouth snaps firmly together.*)

Ellen. (*Laughing*) Mamma's never forgiven him about the baby goat.

Mrs. Callahan. The baby goat —— Whativer was that about?

Ellen. Well, mamma's old Kitty had a kid here one spring, and all the Eyetalians are crazy about young goats in the spring, and Robbie Kelly drove the baby goat over to the Baldocchis' and told Gemma Baldocchi that Mrs. Murphy sent it with her compliments! Mamma went down there—and the yelling—and the screeching! . . . (*She finishes with a high laugh.*)

Mrs. Cahill. (*Shaking her head*) Can you imagine

him doing that, Mrs. Murphy, and getting you mixed up with them dirty *Eyetalians?*

MRS. MURPHY. Yes, Mrs. Cahill, dear, it was humiliatin', it was. Oh, there's no good in the boy.

ELLEN. (*Putting iron away*) I'll tell you what, I don't know that it would hurt that kid to be sent up for a while. He might learn some common sense. He's got no parents, his stepmother is going to marry again, and he says he won't live with his Aunt Lily in Troy. He'll simply go on his way until he kills someone and then it'll be jail.

MRS. MURPHY. (*Hand on teapot*) That's *just* the way it'll be! Have some more tea, Mrs. Cahill?

MRS. CAHILL. No more, thanks, Mrs. Murphy.

MRS. MURPHY. Mrs. Callahan?

MRS. CALLAHAN. No, thanks, dear.

MRS. CAHILL. You'd wonder he *wouldn't* live with his Aunt Lily; she's a fine woman.

MRS. CALLAHAN. She has a good job in the liberry, and he could set there evenings, reading a story out of a book, until she'd be going home.

MRS. CAHILL. She'd give him a good home, and she'd like to have him for company. Lily is a fine ger'rl. The Sisters had her for the Blessed Virgin wanst in their tabloos; she looked very elegant.

MRS. MURPHY. Well, wouldn't you wonder at him? I'll go to the Judge myself one of these days and tell him that if ever there was a lad a few years on the Island would do a world's world of good, me young gallant Robbie Kelly is the lad!

ELLEN. (*Laughing*) Now, Mother!

MRS. MURPHY. (*Pugnaciously*) I *will* so! I'll tell 'um that the boy could have a good home, with a fine ger'rl that's his own mother's sister, Lily Boone, but that he's so wild he wants to run the streets, stealin' goats off of decent, respectable people that has need, God knows, of every penny!

(*The three women nod with vigor.*)

MRS. CALLAHAN. (*Glancing at clock on wall*) I ought to be going, Mrs. Murphy, dear.

MRS. MURPHY. Don't be off so sudden!
MRS. CAHILL. It isn't late.
MRS. MURPHY. What's your hurry?

(*Suddenly there is a great noise in the back yard,— voices, feet upon the porch, and then the door is flung open and the* KELLY KID *bursts in, a thin, tousled, dirty boy of about twelve or fourteen. He is greatly excited, slams the door and drags the ironing-board* [*or some other article of furniture*] *across it, bracing it between him and the door.*)

KELLY KID. (*Yelling between wild sobs, his back to the startled occupants of the room*) You dirty big liar! I never done it—you dirty liar! You can kill me—you can kill me—but you won't send me to jail! I'll get a pistol, and I'll blow your brains out—and I don't care if I *do* go to the chair—I don't care if I do go to the chair—you dirty big liar!

(*The three women are on their feet.*)

MRS. CAHILL. Robbie Kelly!

(MRS. MURPHY *runs to the sink and, wetting the end of a towel, she catches hold of the* KELLY KID *and begins wiping his dirty, tear-stained face.*)

MRS. MURPHY. Here, what's all this to-do? (*As he struggles to get away.*) Here, stand still, now!—What's all this now? This is a fine way to bur'rst in upon a Christian woman! What have you been up to now, Robbie Kelly? I shouldn't wonder if the police are after you again!
KELLY KID. (*Clawing at her hands*) Oh, Mis' Murphy, don't let him get me!
MRS. MURPHY. (*Taking a last rub at his face*) Who?
KELLY KID. Hamilton's after me—the *cop's* after me and Lenny Spillane!
MRS. MURPHY. What have you been doin'?
KELLY KID. Oh, Mis' Murphy, honest to God, I never

done nothin'. It was them big fellers that was foolin' with the switch, and Len and me was just lookin' at what they done ——

Mrs. Cahill. (*Wailing*) My God! There's been a train wreck!

Kelly Kid. No, there wasn't no wreck! But the cop says there might have been, and he says he's going to have me up before Judge Casey—and Judge Casey told me last time he'd send me up to Randall's Island! But I'll *kill* him first! (*He turns his eyes toward the door.*)

Mrs. Callahan. (*Mildly coming up to the* Kelly Kid) It's a pity you wouldn't think of that, Robbie, before now ——

Mrs. Murphy. Yes,—there's some that loved your good mother that thinks maybe you'd be better off for a few years, until you'd be eighteen or so, shut up where you couldn't do any harm.

Mrs. Callahan. (*Interrupting, mildly*) Many's the time I've disputed you about it, Robbie, that you should go to your good aunt, and be a comfort to her and sell a few *Posts* like Martin does, and grow up like a decent man. But no, you'd be stravagin' the neighborhood like a wild Turk that has no God itself, and now look what's in it!

Kelly Kid. I'll go to Aunt Lily—say, if you'll lend me the money for my ticket I'll go, if you'll just get me off this once! Honest I will—I know my way! If you'll get me off with the cop ——

Mrs. Murphy. (*Drily*) So that you can run off wid me goats again!

Kelly Kid. Mrs. Callahan, won't you *please*—won't you please, for the love of God and the Blessed Virgin ——! I'll go to my aunt and I'll help her—I'll split wood for her and run her errands—you'll not be sorry—*honest*—I promise you if I never promised anything in my life ——

Ellen. (*Who has stood the ironing-board up against the wall, out of the way*) For Heaven's sake, Robbie Kelly, why didn't you think of this before? You could have gone to your aunt when your mother died, and entered school there, and tried to make something of yourself. And now you come in with your promises and everything, when the cop's after you, and he's a new cop—nobody likes him, and his hand is against *every*body!

MRS. CAHILL. (*Moving up above table*) You got the Fay boy into trouble, and that was the very first time, and you've been up twice before Judge Casey and you know how mad anything with the railroad makes him ——

(*There is a pause as the women look at each other and shake their heads dubiously. The* KELLY KID *keeps his eye on the door.*)

MRS. CALLAHAN. (*Thoughtfully*) I could go with ye to the Judge, Robbie, but I think he'll send ye up—the third time. I declare if your mother wouldn't rather see you in your grave.

KELLY KID. (*Beginning to cry*) I tell you I never done it.

MRS. CAHILL. You've done enough, God knows!

KELLY KID. But I never done that! And if he takes me and sends me to jail, I'll *tell* him I never done it! He can send me to the chair—because he's a big liar, but I'll tell the Judge that if my mother had lived I'd tell her the same thing—and if I was dyin', I'd tell it —— (*His voice dies away in sobs.*)

ELLEN. (*Taking a handkerchief from her blouse and holding it out to him*) Here—use this on your nose.

(*He is about to take it, when he hears something and whirls about.*)

MRS. CAHILL. (*Who has been looking through the window*) Whisht! There's a cop in the yard!

MRS. CALLAHAN. Saints in the heavens!

MRS. CAHILL. It's Hamilton!

KELLY KID. Don't let him take me! I never done it!

ELLEN. Quick! Come with me —— (*She takes the boy by the shoulder and leads him into the bedroom, closing the door.*)

MRS. MURPHY. What's she going to do with him?

MRS. CALLAHAN. I don't know. Come—let's us be

sittin' natural. That's it, Mrs. Cahill! Be pourin' us some fresh tea, Mrs. Murphy. (MRS. MURPHY *lifts up the teapot.* MRS. CALLAHAN *and* MRS. CAHILL *seat themselves at the table.* MRS. MURPHY *pours the tea into* MRS. CAHILL'S *cup as* MRS. CAHILL *holds it out to her with a trembling hand.* MRS. CALLAHAN, *calmly.*) And what was that you was sayin', Mrs. Murphy?

PYGMALION AND GALATEA

BY W. S. GILBERT

SCENE.—PYGMALION'S *studio. Several classical statues are placed about the room; at the back a raised platform before which curtains are drawn, concealing a statue of* GALATEA.

CHARACTERS: PYGMALION, *an Athenian sculptor.*
GALATEA, *an animated statue.*

(*In speaking blank verse, retain the poetic quality yet give the effect of conversational manner.*)

PYGMALION. (*Bitterly*)
"The thing is but a statue after all!"
Cynisca little thought that in those words
She touched the keynote of my discontent—
True, I have powers denied other men;
Give me a block of senseless marble—Well,
I'm a magician and it rests with me
To say what kernel lies within its shell;
It shall contain a man, a woman, a child,
A dozen men and women if I will.
So far the gods and I run neck and neck,
Nay, so far I can beat them at their trade;
I am no bungler—all the men *I* make
Are straight-limbed fellows, each magnificent
In the perfection of his manly grace;

I make no crook-backs—all my men are gods,
My women goddesses, in outward form.
But there's my tether—I can go so far,
And go no farther—at that point I stop,
To curse the bonds that hold me sternly back.
To curse the arrogance of those proud gods,
Who say, " Thou shalt be greatest among men,
And yet infinitesimally small!"

GALATEA. (*From behind curtain*) Pygmalion!

PYGMALION. (*After a pause*)   Who called?

GALATEA.   Pygmalion!

(PYGMALION *tears away curtain and discovers* GALATEA *alive.*)

PYGMALION. Ye gods! It lives!

GALATEA.   Pygmalion!

PYGMALION.   It speaks!
  I have my prayer! My Galatea breathes!

GALATEA.
  Where am I? Let me speak, Pygmalion;
  Give me thy hand—both hands—how soft and warm!
  Whence came I? (*Descends.*)

PYGMALION.   Why, from yonder pedestal.

GALATEA. That pedestal! Ah yes, I recollect.
  There was a time when it was part of me.

PYGMALION. That time has passed forever, thou art now
  A living, breathing woman, excellent
  In every attribute of womankind.

GALATEA. Where am I, then?

PYGMALION.   Why, born into the world
  By miracle.

GALATEA. Is this the world?

PYGMALION. It is.

GALATEA. This room?

PYGMALION.
      This room is a portion of a house;
The house stands in a grove, the grove itself
Is one of many, many hundred groves
In Athens.

GALATEA.   And is Athens then the world?

PYGMALION. To an Athenian—yes ——

GALATEA. And I am one?

PYGMALION. By birth and parentage, not by descent.

GALATEA. But how came I to be?

PYGMALION. Well,—let me see.
Oh,—you were quarried in Pentelicus;
I modelled you in clay—my artisans
Then roughed you out in marble—I, in turn
Brought my artistic skill to bear on you,
And made you what you are—in all but life—
The gods completed what I had begun,
And gave the only gift I could not give.

GALATEA. Then this is life?

PYGMALION. It is.

GALATEA. And not long since
I was a cold dull stone. I recollect
That by some means I knew that I was stone,
That was the first dull gleam of consciousness,
I became conscious of a chilly self,
A cold, immovable identity,
I knew that I was stone, and knew no more;
Then, by an imperceptible advance,

Came the dim evidence of outer things,
Seen—darkly and imperfectly—yet seen—
The walls surrounded me, and I, alone,
That pedestal—that curtain—then a voice
That called on Galatea! At that word,
Which seemed to shake my marble to the core,
That which was dim before, came evident.
Sounds, that had hummed around me, indistinct,
Vague, meaningless—seemed to resolve themselves
Into a language I could understand;
I felt my frame pervaded with a glow
That seemed to thaw my marble into flesh;
Its cold hard substance throbbed with active life,
My limbs grew supple, and I moved—I lived;
Lived in the ecstasy of newborn life;
Lived in the love of him that fashioned me;
Lived in a thousand tangled thoughts of hope,
Love, gratitude, thoughts that resolved themselves
Into one word, that word, Pygmalion!

(*Kneels to him.*)

PYGMALION. I have no words to tell thee of my joy,
O woman—perfect in thy loveliness.

GALATEA. What is that word? Am I a woman?

PYGMALION. Yes.

GALATEA. Art thou a woman?

PYGMALION. No, I am a man.

GALATEA. What *is* a man?

PYGMALION. A being strongly framed,
To wait on woman, and protect her from
All ills that strength and courage can avert;
To work and toil for her, that she may rest;
To weep and mourn for her, that she may laugh;
To fight and die for her, that she may live!

GALATEA. (*After a pause*) I'm glad I am a woman.

(*Takes his hand—he leads her down* L.)

PYGMALION. So am I.

(*They sit.*)

*WHAT MEN LIVE BY

From an Adaptation of the Story by Leo Tolstoi

BY VIRGINIA CHURCH

SCENE.—*A corner of the basement occupied by Simon, the cobbler, and* MATRENA, *his wife. In the* L. *wall is a hearth where* MATRENA *cooks the meals. Two old chairs are near the hearth, also a table.*)

CHARACTERS: MATRENA.
ANNA MALOSKA, *a widow.*

(MATRENA *takes an iron pot from the table and hangs it before the fire. She busies herself preparing to cook porridge. There is a knock.*)

MATRENA. Come in. (*A comely woman of middle age enters. She is rather overdressed in poor clothes that strive to imitate the rich.*) Ah, Anna, is it you? Come in.

ANNA. Who was it went out?

MATRENA. Simon has gone to buy a sheepskin. Sit down. Is it cold out?

ANNA. (*Sitting and throwing back her wraps*) Bitter cold. It was on just such a day my poor husband caught pneumonia.

* Copyright, 1924, Atlantic Monthly Press, Inc.

MATRENA. (*Sitting on other side of the fire*) I do hope Simon won't catch cold and I do hope the sheepskin-seller won't cheat him. That man of mine is a regular simpleton.

ANNA. They all are, poor dears!

MATRENA. Simon never cheats a soul himself, yet a little child can lead him by the nose. It's time he was back; he had only a short way to go.

ANNA. If it were poor dear Ivan, I should know he had stopped for a glass of vodka.

MATRENA. (*Walking to the window and looking out*) I hope he hasn't gone making merry, that rascal of mine.

ANNA. Ah, Matrena, they are all rascals. Ivan drank himself into a stupor every evening; then he would come home and beat me, and beat little Fifi, my dog; but I have to remember that he was a man and men are like that. I shall never be happy again, now that he is in his grave. (*She weeps.*)

MATRENA. (*Patting her shoulder*) There, there, poor Anna!

ANNA. (*Brightening*) Do you like my hat?

MATRENA. Aye, aye, it is very tasty; though, if I might say, a trifle youthful.

ANNA. Why shouldn't a woman cheat Father Time if she can? He's the only man she can get even with. He liked my hat.

MATRENA. Ivan?

ANNA. Oh, no, the poor dear died without seeing it. I mean Martin Pakhom. I just met him at the door and he said, "Good day, Anna, what a beautiful hat that is you're wearing!"

MATRENA. They say Martin drinks like a trout.

ANNA. Ah, they all do, poor dears. I must go on. Fifi will be wanting his supper, though neither of us has eaten anything since poor Ivan died. Fifi is so affectionate. We both cry an hour every morning.

MATRENA. Poor Anna!

ANNA. Won't you walk a way with me?

MATRENA. Simon went out with all our clothes upon him and left me nothing to wear. Besides, I must get his supper ready, and clean out my sleeping-room.

ANNA. (*Rising*) I wish *I* had someone to get supper for. (*Going to door.*) Matrena, Martin said something rather pointed just now.
MATRENA. What did he say, Anna?
ANNA. He said, " Marriage is a lottery! "
MATRENA. Aye, aye, so it is.
ANNA. I was just wondering——
MATRENA. Yes?
ANNA. I was wondering if Martin were thinking of taking a chance. Good-bye, Matrena.
MATRENA. Good-bye, Anna. [ANNA *goes out.*

Complete copies of the plays from which these scenes are made can be supplied by the publishers

Miscellaneous Business

When playing a character part, you will, of course, walk, sit, stand and gesture in a manner which suggests that character. At other times you must appear natural and at ease,—two very difficult things to do, considering their apparent simplicity.

Smooth, rhythmical, well co-ordinated movement with no waste motion is the ideal. There is no better exercise for gaining poise and balance in walking than the old practise of carrying a book on the head. Let the legs swing easily from the hips (not at the knees), and walk on one line (not on two lines). Negotiate steps in the same way, taking the first step with the upstage foot.

Before sitting, do not turn to see that the chair is in place behind you, but step close enough to it so that you feel it with the back of your leg, and then let yourself down into it, making one leg bear your weight until you touch the seat of the chair. Women should keep their ankles together and not allow their knees to spread. For them there is less knee-crossing than is permissible in even informal occasions in real life, but when it may be done, be certain that it is the knees that are crossed, *not* the legs!

When rising, sit well forward in the chair first, then lift your weight on your legs; don't pull yourself out by clutching the arms of the chair.

Selection of chairs and davenports should be made with consideration of the actor's use as well as for appearance. Many of the most modern, luxuriously comfortable pieces cannot be used at all because of the difficulty of getting into and out of them with an inconspicuous grace.

Standing quietly will not be quite so difficult if you remember to keep listening to and watching what is going on in the play. Be alive and alert, but not rigid; relax, but don't slouch.

Kneel on the downstage knee. Women wearing long or full skirts may need to free the costume by lifting it ever so slightly with one hand as she kneels.

In falling, let the body relax, then slip down, the ankle, knee, hip and shoulder reaching the floor in rapid succession.

Eating, drinking and smoking must all be carefully timed so that the business does not interfere with the lines but the two processes must be synchronized perfectly. Rehearse thoroughly with real properties and avoid embarrassment in the actual performance.

The technique of laughing and crying is really not hard to master. In speaking, the breath is inhaled and exhaled quietly and evenly. In laughing and crying it is inhaled audibly in little gasps, and exhaled in a series of jerky explosions. Any words that are uttered during this process must be emitted of course on the outgoing breath.

Scenes involving the use of the telephone should not be too hurried, so as to fail to create an illusion of reality. Imagine you hear another voice at the other end of the line, allowing time for the person to speak. If necessary, make up the words he might be saying, and be sure to show response to what he has said to you.

*MARY THE FIRST

BY RACHEL CROTHERS

(Prologue from the play " Mary the Third ")

SCENE.—*It is the year 1870. The stage is hung in dark curtains, the center is lighted. An old mahogany sofa, upholstered in black haircloth, is the only furniture.*

CHARACTERS: MARY, *a girl of twenty.*
WILLIAM, *a tall good-looking fellow.*

(MARY *is discovered seated on the sofa, fanning herself nervously with her diminutive fan, waiting and watching. Shyness and modesty are her manner. Her movements are graceful and coy and mincing,— full of a conscious charm. An orchestra from a seductive distance is playing an enticing polka. Suddenly,* WILLIAM *comes quickly into the scene.*)

MARY. Good gracious! How did you know I was here?

WILLIAM. You told me you would be.

MARY. I didn't! The idea of you thinking such a thing!

WILLIAM. (*Heavy, honest and simple minded*) I thought you said as soon as you finished that dance with Hiram, you'd come in here.

MARY. I may have said I *might* but I didn't say I *would*.

WILLIAM. Well, I hoped you would.

MARY. Where's Lucy? I didn't suppose you'd be looking for *me* when you were dancing with *her*.

WILLIAM. I finished.

MARY. Aren't you going to dance this one with her?

* Copyright, 1923, Rachel Crothers

It's your favorite polka and *now* no one in the world dances the polka so well as Lucy, of course.

WILLIAM. No one but you.

MARY. Oh, that's what you *used* to say. But you can't say that any more. Go on. Don't keep her waiting.

WILLIAM. Who's waiting for *you?*

MARY. I won't tell you.

WILLIAM. It's Hiram. How many times have you danced with him?

MARY. How do I know?

WILLIAM. Every other dance. Is this his, too?

MARY. I'm not dancing with anybody this time. I'm just sitting here resting. It's so sweet and quiet. Listen! Isn't the music sweet? I shall always think of you, William, when I hear that music. We've danced to it so many, many times. Oh, I oughtn't to have said that.

WILLIAM. Why not?

MARY. I mustn't say those things now. And you must go. . . . This is really good-bye, William, isn't it?

WILLIAM. No, it's not! Unless *you* want it to be.

MARY. Oh, *me!* Don't say me. What have I to do with it?

WILLIAM. Everything. It all depends on you whether it's good-bye or not.

MARY. Then of course it's good-bye. Dear, dear little Lucy! I hope you'll be happy with her, William. Goodbye. (*Giving him her hand daintily, and drawing it away at once.*)

WILLIAM. What are you goin' on like this for? Nothing's going to be any different for you and me.

MARY. Oh, do you suppose for a minute she'll ever let you dance with me again?

WILLIAM. She can't help herself.

MARY. Oh, you don't know her as I do. I love Lucy very, *very* dearly. She doesn't mean to be ——

WILLIAM. What?

MARY. Nothing. I ought not to have said that.

WILLIAM. Said what? What are you hiding?

MARY. Oh, I'm not *hiding* anything about Lucy. Good gracious! I wouldn't have you think *that* for *any*thing. Oh, dear. Oh, dear! Rather than have you think that, I'll tell you right out what was on my mind. I only meant that under her sweet little purring ways she's really very, *very* strong and stubborn and always gets what she wants. She won't let you be my dear old friend any more. . . .

WILLIAM. She can't stop that.

MARY. You mustn't say that. It's all over now.

WILLIAM. It never would have been over if you hadn't preferred Hiram and his money.

MARY. Oh, don't blame me. But it *is* over. So let's not talk about it. Let's just be happy for a moment here . . . in this sweet corner where we've sat so many, many times.

WILLIAM. We'll sit here again sometimes, too. (*Trying to take her hand which she finally allows him to do after a modest struggle.*)

MARY. Oh, never, *never!* You ought to know that, William. You ought to know that I will be loyal to Lucy always—above everything. . . . Dear, dear little Lucy. I must be true to her.

WILLIAM. What about being true to me? You can't throw me away like an old shoe. . . .

MARY. (*Turning away and brushing a tear from her cheek*) Good-bye, William.—You *must* go.

WILLIAM. I won't go until you tell me just what you mean and just how you're feeling.

MARY. No—no—it's too late.

WILLIAM. It's not too late. I'm not tied up yet. . . .

MARY. Oh, no—no—Lucy!

WILLIAM. I've got more money than Hiram has now. More than he ever will have. Granddad left me rich, Mary. I'm a rich man now. If I thought you still cared for me the way you once did—nothing could hold me back from getting you.

MARY. Oh, William, William, you mustn't say that. (*Taking the rose from her hair, smelling it and holding it to her lips.*) Take this and keep it and look at it sometimes when it's faded and think of me. Perhaps I'll be faded, too. Isn't it pretty?

WILLIAM. Not half so pretty as you are.

MARY. Oh!

WILLIAM. Your cheek is much softer and pinker.

MARY. How can you say such a thing! It couldn't be. See. Look! (*Holding the rose to her cheek and bending near him. He kisses her cheek.*) Oh—how could you! How could you, William! Oh,—you're hurting my arm! Oh, William,—you mustn't!

WILLIAM. I won't let anybody else have you. Are you engaged to Hiram?

MARY. Oh, what does it matter?

WILLIAM. I never have loved any other girl. I never will.

MARY. And do you think I've ever loved any other man? Oh, I ought not to have said that. But I will say it, just this once before we part forever. I loved you as no girl ever loved a man. (WILLIAM *bends over her hands and holds them to his lips.*) We must be brave, William, and say good-bye.

WILLIAM. (*Kneeling before her, his head bowed in her hands*) I can't—I can't—don't ask it.

MARY. It's too late. You're pledged to another. You must be true to her and live a beautiful life, William.

WILLIAM. I'm not going to do it. You're my fate. I'll blow my brains out if you don't marry me. I'll kill anybody else that gets you.

MARY. (*Sobbing*) But fate is parting us.

WILLIAM. Look here. I'll have the horses ready in an hour. You go home and put on your riding habit and meet me at the crossroads in an hour.

MARY. No, no, William. I couldn't—I couldn't.

WILLIAM. (*Still on his knees*) You've got to. We can't let life treat us like this. We've got to take hold of things. Nothing can stop us. This is meant to be.

MARY. Then it would be wrong to let anything separate us. It's stronger than we are, William. Eternal and beautiful like the stars. But, oh, I can't do it, William. Never—never in this world can I do it. I'm not sure that it would be right. I'll be behind the oak tree. It's bigger than the maple.

WILLIAM. (*Getting up*) You angel!

MARY. Don't you bring Fleetfoot. I'm afraid of her. Bring Silver Star. Will you love me forever?

WILLIAM. Forever and ever.
MARY. In this world and the next?
WILLIAM. Longer than eternity.
MARY. There never has been a love as great as this. I feel it. I know it. Oh, William, I love you so! I love you! (*They are locked in each other's arms as the light fades.*)

*GLAMOUR

BY PERCIVAL WILDE

SCENE.—*The dressing-room of* RODERICK VANE, *star, in a Broadway theatre. A door, back, leads to the stage. Down* L. *is a door which opens on the hallway.*

CHARACTERS: A DRESSER.
A GIRL.
AN ACTOR.

(MR. VANE *is seated before his dressing table, his* DRESSER *hovering about.*)

DRESSER. She insists on seeing you. (*The left-hand door opens quietly.*) She absolutely insists.
GIRL. I do, Mr. Vane! I absolutely do! (*He rises and looks at her.*) Mr. Vane, you were marvelous tonight!
ACTOR. (*Chuckling*) Did you notice it, too?
GIRL. You were marvelous! Marvelous! (*She takes a step toward him, puts her hand over her heart, totters, and collapses at full length on the floor.*)
ACTOR. (*Going to her quickly*) Good Heavens! The poor child's fainted—and I was joking with her! Harry, bring me some water! Be quick, Harry! Water! . . .
DRESSER. Here you are, sir.
ACTOR. (*Turning her on her back*) Poor thing!

* Copyright, 1935, Percival Wilde

She's probably half-starved. I know what it's like to walk the streets looking for a job.

DRESSER. She looks well nourished to me, sir.

ACTOR. What do *you* know about it? Are *you* ever hungry? (*He has raised her to a half-sitting position.*) Here, drink this! (*She pushes the glass away feebly.*) Harry, she doesn't want it!

GIRL. Where am I? (*Still supported by* VANE'S *arm, she strikes a pose.*)

> I do remember well where I should be,
> And there I am.

"Romeo and Juliet." (*She speaks the lines, following them with the title of the play. The men stare at her. She takes the glass.*) Is this the place from which you drank? I want to drink from the same place. . . . Shakespeare wrote something like that, but I don't remember how it goes. (*She drinks some water. She smiles. She rises, accepting* VANE'S *automatically proffered help, and accepting also the handbag she carries and which he retrieves for her.*) Thank you, Mr. Vane. (*She finds a mirror and a lipstick in the bag and begins to primp.*) That was my faint. Didn't you like it? They said it couldn't be distinguished from the real thing at the Troy Little Theatre. Ayuh. Would you like me to faint for you again, Mr. Vane? (*She begins to stagger, turning, and threatening to collapse in any direction.*)

DRESSER. Look out, sir! She may fall on you, and there's a matinee tomorrow!

GIRL. (*Continuing to gyrate*) If I fall on him, I won't hurt him.

DRESSER. (*Grasping her*) I've got her, sir! I've got her! Mr. Vane, if you'll open the door ——

GIRL. Stop! Stop, or I'll scream! Would you like to hear me scream, Mr. Vane? Everybody says it's bloodcurdling.

ACTOR. Please don't.

GIRL. Why not?

ACTOR. A woman's screams coming from my dressing-room might create an unfortunate impression.

GIRL. (*Much interested*) Would they? Honest? . . . Would you rather hear me recite?

ACTOR. Is that bloodcurdling, too?

GIRL. Just listen. (*In a decidedly amateurish manner, lengthening out every " O," she declaims.*)

> O, woe! O woful, woful, woful day!
> Most lamentable day, most woful day,
> That ever, ever I did yet behold!
> O day! O day! O day! O hateful day!
> Never was seen so black a day as this:
> O woful day! O woful day!

(*She stops, and looks at him smiling, awaiting approbation.*)

ACTOR. (*Puffing at his cigar and gazing at her sharply*) It must have been the worst weather they ever had in Troy.

*THE AFFAIRS OF MEN

(Scene 1)

BY WARREN BECK

SCENE.—*Part of a waiting-room in a railway station in Chicago. The time is late afternoon.*

CHARACTERS: THE NEW YORK BOY.
THE SAN FRANCISCO BOY.

(*The* NEW YORK BOY *comes in. He is burly and ruddy. His clothing bears the marks of long hours of slouching in the seat of a day coach. Having placed his baggage near a bench, he examines and crumples an empty cigarette package, looks around and tosses the empty package away and goes out. From the other side, the* SAN FRANCISCO BOY *wanders in. He is slim and trimmer in appearance than the* NEW YORK BOY.

* Copyright, 1931, Walter H. Baker Company

His clothes are also amazingly wrinkled. He sits down aimlessly next to the NEW YORK BOY'S *seat, dropping his baggage in front of him to furnish a footrest.* NEW YORK *returns, frowns critically at* SAN FRANCISCO, *sits down and begins to open his fresh package of cigarettes.* SAN FRANCISCO *also gets out a cigarette, but cannot find a match.*)

SAN FRANCISCO. Got a match, partner? (NEW YORK *hands over his matches in gloomy silence and waits somewhat suspiciously until they are returned.*) Thanks.

(NEW YORK *replies with a grunt. They smoke in silence.*)

NEW YORK. Traveling?
SAN FRANCISCO. Sure. Are you?
NEW YORK. Yeh. (*After some pondering.*) Going far?
SAN FRANCISCO. I'll say. New York.
NEW YORK. New York? Well!
SAN FRANCISCO. Ever been there?
NEW YORK. Have I ever been there? Have I ever been in little old New York? Fellow, I've lived there all my life—until two days ago.
SAN FRANCISCO. Is that so?
NEW YORK. Yeah. Great place—New York.
SAN FRANCISCO. That's what they tell me.
NEW YORK. You've never been there?
SAN FRANCISCO. No. I've never been east before. Lived all my life in San Francisco.
NEW YORK. Huh? Why, that's where I'm bound for.
SAN FRANCISCO. What—'Frisco?
NEW YORK. Yeah.
SAN FRANCISCO. (*After a brief pause for thought*) Funny, our meeting this way. Just as if we're trading places.
NEW YORK. It is kind of queer.

(*They smoke in silence for a moment.*)

SAN FRANCISCO. This Chicago is a rotten town!

NEW YORK. You said it. It's terrible!

SAN FRANCISCO. 'Frisco! There's a real place! Partner, you're going to a pretty swell town, I'll tell you.

NEW YORK. You didn't pick out the worst burg in the world when you started to New York. There's only one New York, you know.

SAN FRANCISCO. Yes, I know. I reckon you must have been sorry to have to leave.

NEW YORK. (*Judiciously*) Well, no—I didn't exactly have to leave, see? I just got tired of things—same old job, same old people, same old streets. I thought I'd look around a little bit. Always had intended to go west some day—so finally I just up and left.

SAN FRANCISCO. Same here exactly—except the other way round.

NEW YORK. Of course I like New York. That's only natural—anybody would.

SAN FRANCISCO. I guess everybody likes their own home town best.

NEW YORK. But a man can't always stick in the same town. A young fellow, especially, has got to show some life these days if he expects to get ahead.

SAN FRANCISCO. Sure. That's just what I've always thought. I've said so lots of times. Take for instance young fellows like you and I. We have to be careful or we'll settle down in a rut, and then where would we be?

NEW YORK. You're right. You can't get nowhere in a rut.

SAN FRANCISCO. That's the truth—it's kind of hard, though, for a fellow to pull up stakes when he's lived in a place all his life, like I have in 'Frisco.

NEW YORK. Yes, or like I have in New York. (*Fervently.*) I sure did hate to leave that burg!

SAN FRANCISCO. I know just how you feel. But I reckon it's got to be done sometime or other.

NEW YORK. You said it! Just like a man in New York says to me—it's enterprise that counts. If you never try nothing new, you don't get nowhere.

SAN FRANCISCO. That's a fact. You can't just sit

around waiting for luck to hit you in the face. You've got to go where the opportunities are.

NEW YORK. That's right. I've always said that. A young man, especially, has to go where the opportunities are.

SAN FRANCISCO. Sure!

(*They are silent a moment, each reflecting respectfully upon his own insight.*)

NEW YORK. You don't know anything about the restaurant business in 'Frisco, do you?

SAN FRANCISCO. Not a thing. I ate in 'em, that's all. Is that what you've been in—the restaurant business?

NEW YORK. (*Airily*) Oh, yes. Several years.

SAN FRANCISCO. (*Awed*) Did you own a restaurant in New York?

NEW YORK. (*Slowly*) No—I didn't own it.

SAN FRANCISCO. Just worked in it?

NEW YORK. Yep.

SAN FRANCISCO. What's your specialty?

NEW YORK. Well, lately I've been cook's helper.

SAN FRANCISCO. Oh! (*He is obviously disappointed.*)

NEW YORK. (*Briskly*) I expect I can pick up a job in 'Frisco, all right.

SAN FRANCISCO. Well, of course, there's lots of Chinese cooks in 'Frisco.

NEW YORK. (*Soberly*) I never thought of that.— In your line of work—do they give you much competition?

SAN FRANCISCO. No, they don't give me no competition. (*Proudly.*)

NEW YORK. (*Impressed*) You must be in something pretty good.

SAN FRANCISCO. Well, it's not so bad.

NEW YORK. (*Further impressed*) You're not a salesman, are you?

SAN FRANCISCO. Oh, no. (*After a pause.*) I'm— I'm a elevator operator.

NEW YORK. (*Eloquently*) Oh! Well, they have

more elevators in New York than all the rest of the country put together.

San Francisco. Yes, that's what I thought, in all those skyscrapers.

New York. You said it.

San Francisco. I don't know, though; I was thinking I might get into another line. Elevators are all right —it's clean—and you get to meet the public. But some days it gets awful monotonous.

New York. Up and down, up and down, huh?

San Francisco. Sure. I've been thinking that maybe New York would give me a chance at something different.

New York. Well, there's all kinds of jobs in New York—if you can find 'em!

San Francisco. Yes, I reckon it's the same everywhere. Plenty of jobs—if you can find them.

New York. Breaking into something different—it's not so easy, though. That's why I thought I'd pick up a cook's job in San Francisco until I got onto things and had a chance to look around.

San Francisco. I had the same idea—thought I'd stay in the elevator line in New York a while—but not too long.

New York. I don't want to discourage you, 'Frisco, but there's a friend of mine in New York, an elevator operator—he got laid off, and he had a hard time finding another elevator job.

San Francisco. Is that so?

New York. Yeh.

San Francisco. That sounds bad.

New York. It's a funny thing. New York's a big place, but at that there seems to be two men for every job. That's one of the reasons I made up my mind to strike out for the West.

San Francisco. Well, partner, right now there's plenty of men out of work in 'Frisco, I can tell you.

New York. Is that right?

San Francisco. Sure!

New York. Why, a fellow told me that there was lots of jobs everywhere in California.

San Francisco. Maybe he meant in '49. . . . You don't suppose I'd have left if there was plenty of jobs, do you?

(*Again they smoke and reflect.*)

New York. I got a knot in the back of my neck from trying to sleep curled up on a seat.

San Francisco. Wait till you get to 'Frisco. That's three nights more. I twisted around so many ways on that seat that I reckon I'll need a month to get straightened out again.

New York. It's not so bad if you get a double seat and can stretch out your legs.

San Francisco. Sure, that helps. But by the time you get to 'Frisco you'll know you've been traveling, partner.

New York. (*Getting up and pacing back and forth impatiently*) Gee, don't this waiting get on your nerves?

San Francisco. Sure.

New York. I wish—oh, well, I'll soon be on my way.

San Francisco. When do you go?

New York. Half an hour—five-forty—on the Golden Gate Limited.

San Francisco. The Golden Gate! Boy, you'll open your eyes when you see that. Gee!

New York. When does your train leave?

San Francisco. Six o'clock.

New York. Six o'clock—you'll be in New York this time to-morrow.

San Francisco. I reckon so.

New York. (*Sighing grandly*) Well, we're here today and gone tomorrow, eh, 'Frisco?

Complete copies of the plays from which these scenes were made can be supplied by the publishers

Speaking Conversationally

It would seem that to speak conversationally might be one of the easiest things to do. It is not. Too often the young player, conscious of the fact that he is acting a part, memorizes his lines *as speeches* and then merely recites what he has learned.

Listen to the talk of people about you. Notice how easily it comes? how unpremeditatedly? Notice the characteristics of such speech,—the variations in speed, —the pauses,—the slides, or inflections, in the voice,—the different ways of emphasis.

During the time an actor is analyzing his character and *studying* (not learning) his part, he may quite consciously experiment with these elements of interpretation but, in the end, he has so mastered the use of them that they seem to spring naturally, simply and spontaneously from his thought. Talk on the stage should sound like talk, not like a lecture.

Bulkalov, the Russian director, warns actors lest they "let the lines run ahead of the thought". Think what you are saying, then you will seem to be saying what you think.

These scenes represent simple, everyday situations. Project your whole character portrayal so that you can be heard, understood, and felt to the farthest rows of seats,—but be certain that your *thinking* keeps abreast of your lines.

*GRANDMA PULLS THE STRING
(Scene 1)

BY EDITH BARNARD DELANO AND DAVID CARB

SCENE.—*A living-room.*

CHARACTERS: MRS. CUMMINGS.
   NONA, *her married daughter.*
   JULIA, *her second daughter.*

(MRS. CUMMINGS *is discovered, brushing tables, straightening chairs, and generally touching up the room.* NONA *enters.*)

NONA. (*Grinning mischievously*) Has the gentleman announced that he is going to snatch your second daughter from the arms of her loving family tonight, Mother?

MRS. CUMMINGS. Certainly not. Don't be absurd, Nona. But—well, after all, during the entire two months he's been rushing Julia. And I do think she's—well, fond of him. And since he has to go home tomorrow—well, there it is! (*Now she looks directly at* NONA *for the first time, and speaks as though she is glad to change the subject.*) Why, Nona! What a *beautiful* coat!

NONA. (*Twirling about*) Isn't it wonderful? George made a lucky guess on the market. I'm crazy about it.

MRS. CUMMINGS. It looks mighty expensive.

NONA. Oh, George is a good sport—when he's properly directed.

MRS. CUMMINGS. (*Wistfully*) I wish Julia had a fur coat.

NONA. She'll have a dozen—if she catches Bill Thornton. (*She takes off the coat and throws it on a chair.*)

* Copyright, 1926, Edith Barnard Delano and David Carb

Mrs. Cummings. Oh, Nona! Catches! (Nona *shrugs and grins.*) You grow sillier every day!

Nona. (*Swiftly embracing her mother, laughing*) Nervous?

Mrs. Cummings. No, tired. We made a whole dress today.

Nona. Poor little mother.

Mrs. Cummings. When you have a daughter of your own you'll know how it feels to ——

Nona. Oh, Mother, you're so sentimental!

Julia. (*Entering in time to hear* Nona) That's the right word, Nona, "sentimental." I've had to put up with this sort of thing for days! You'd think I was the ugliest duckling in the world and a million years old,—everyone's so overjoyed at the mere possibility of getting rid of me. There's nothing in it, anyway. Just because Bill is going away tomorrow and is coming to say good-bye ——

Nona. (*Patting her—and* Julia *moves away from the pat*) Don't let it get under your skin, old girl! George and I had to go through the same sort of thing! (*Continues brightly.*) You *look* lovely!

Julia. (*Smiling doubtfully*) Like me?

Nona. Peach of a dress. Men adore blue.

Julia. (*Confidentially*) What shall I do, Nona?

(Mrs. Cummings *is doing more things to the room.*)

Nona. Grab him.

Julia. You, too! (*She turns away.*)

Nona. He *is* going to propose, isn't he?

Julia. (*Flaming out at her*) You're as big a fool as the others!

Nona. (*Ambiguously*) That's what I was led to believe.

Julia. He's going away tomorrow and he's coming tonight to say good-bye. That's all there is to it.

Nona. (*Teasing*) Nothing else.

Julia. I did think you would understand!

Nona. (*Relenting—almost tenderly*) I do, dear— I do.

JULIA. Then for goodness' sake help me! (*Blurting out her trouble.*) I want to see him alone. And Dick is studying in the dining-room, and Grandma is going to insist on coming in here.

NONA. Why? She likes the dining-room better.

JULIA. Of course she does. She always says the light is bad in here. But tonight, ever since dinner, she's been complaining—the dining-room's chilly. She just wants to be in here with us. And somehow she'll manage to get here.

NONA. Can't you take him out somewhere?

JULIA. How can I? That dowdy old coat of mine ——

NONA. He's seen it before!

JULIA. But—it's his last night.

NONA. He'll be thinking of you, not your coat.

JULIA. But his last sight of me must be—e—well, *not* a sloppy, shapeless, out-of-date, faded ——

MRS. CUMMINGS. (*Coming forward*) Your coat isn't as bad as all that, my dear! And what does it matter?

JULIA. It matters tremendously.

MRS. CUMMINGS. Wear mine!

JULIA. Oh, Mother!

MRS. CUMMINGS. Look what George gave Nona. (*She holds up the fur coat.*)

JULIA. Oh, how gorgeous!

NONA. Pretty nifty? He surprised me with it tonight.

JULIA. How did he know which kind you wanted?

NONA. Oh, I have a little way of taking him window-shopping! (*She is very proud of her foresight—she knows how to manage husbands.*)

JULIA. (*Stroking it*) A dream—a dream coat—Nona, could I? May I try it on?

(NONA *holds the coat and* JULIA *slips into it.*)

NONA. You look like a million dollars!
JULIA. I feel like Standard Oil!

*GRANDMA PULLS THE STRING
(Scene 2)
BY EDITH BARNARD DELANO AND DAVID CARB

SCENE.—*Same as Scene 1.*

CHARACTERS: NONA.
HILDEGARDE, *her younger sister.*

(HILDEGARDE, *in a state of suppressed excitement, is standing in the middle of the living-room studying the effect of her re-arrangement. With its " broken" speech, neither character should anticipate the interruption.*)

HILDEGARDE. Sister Nona, come in here a minute! I want to ask you something.
NONA. (*Entering*) Why the heavy darkness? (*She moves toward lamp.*)
HILDEGARDE. Oh, don't! I—don't you think the darkness is—nice?
NONA. Why, yes! As darkness goes. But what's the idea?
HILDEGARDE. It's so romantic!
NONA. Romantic——! You darling child, what on earth——
HILDEGARDE. It makes the room seem like a love bower.
NONA. A love——! Why, Hildegarde!
HILDEGARDE. (*Proudly*) *I* fixed the lights this way!
NONA. You! *Your* love bower!
HILDEGARDE. (*Impatient with her denseness*) Of course not! Not mine! Julia's!
NONA. Julia's! Soft lights—where's the music?
HILDEGARDE. (*Solemnly, rather regretfully*) There isn't any music.
NONA. Do you mean to say that Julia is staging——?

* Copyright, 1926, Edith Barnard Delano and David Carb

HILDEGARDE. Sh—sh——! Julia doesn't know anything at all about it.

NONA. Then wh——

HILDEGARDE. (*Blurting it out*) She's dressing up in a brand-new blue chiffon she and mother made today, and the lace handkerchief Grandma gave me, and Mother's amber beads and the silk stockings you gave her for Christmas, and she's got new slippers with silver buckles on them, and she's got a new vanity case that looks like solid gold, and——

NONA. Hold on—hold on! What's it all about? What's Julia dolling up that way for?

HILDEGARDE. Mr. Thornton got well quicker'n he thought he would and he's got to go back home to Springfield tomorrow, and this is his last night here and we think he'll ask Julia's hand in marriage——

NONA. Ask Julia's hand——! Oh—oh—— (*She bursts into laughter.*)

HILDEGARDE. Sister Nona! Don't—don't——

NONA. Ask Julia's hand! (*She continues to laugh.*)

HILDEGARDE. Well, that's what gentlemen do when they propose!

NONA. Who told you so?

HILDEGARDE. I *know* it. (*A pause.* NONA *stares at* HILDEGARDE, *bites her lip.*) They kneel down and beg——

NONA. Kneel down! You Victorian child——!

HILDEGARDE. (*Pointing*) He'll kneel on that very cushion. I put it there so's he could.

NONA. (*Laughing*) Oh, my dear—my dear—my dear! What on earth makes you think he'll kneel?

HILDEGARDE. (*Proudly*) Mr. Thornton is a gentleman. He will do it the way a gentleman should.

NONA. And so you arranged all this—this scenery.

HILDEGARDE. (*Hurt*) I wanted to help.

> Lives of great men all remind us
> We can make our lives sublime!

NONA. Longfellow! My stars! (*To* HILDEGARDE.) So you turned the lights out and ——

HILDEGARDE. And put the cushion on the floor, so he won't get his trousers dusty when he kneels at her feet.

NONA. They still grow that young! (*Gathering the child in her arms.*) You darling! Men don't kneel any more.

HILDEGARDE. Men *do!* And Mr. Thornton will. Because that's the right way to do it.

NONA. How do you know he will do it at all, standing, or—kneeling?

HILDEGARDE. (*Importantly*) Oh, we *know.*

NONA. Did he broadcast his intention?

HILDEGARDE. Of course not.

NONA. Listen, dear. That's not the way it's done. The man says, "Gee, you look good to me!" And the girl says, "What d'you say we hitch up?"

HILDEGARDE. (*Squirming out of her sister's embrace*) They don't! They don't!

NONA. Nowadays they ——

HILDEGARDE. (*Defiantly*) They kneel at their ladylove's feet and pray her ——

NONA. What a picture! (*She laughs.*) Imagine him ——! Poor Julia!

HILDEGARDE. I hate you!

NONA. Why, Hildegarde ——!

HILDEGARDE. Nothing is sacred to you! You make fun of everything sacred. I—hate you! (*In tears she runs from the room.* NONA *follows her after a thoughtful pause.*)

*GRANDMA PULLS THE STRING

(Scene 3)

BY EDITH BARNARD DELANO AND DAVID CARB

SCENE.—*Same as close of Scene 2.*

CHARACTERS: HILDEGARDE.
JULIA.
MR. THORNTON.

* Copyright, 1926, Edith Barnard Delano and David Carb

(HILDEGARDE *and* JULIA *in living-room.* HILDEGARDE *starts to leave.*)

JULIA. You don't have to go, Hildegarde. (*Crosses and picks up cushion from the floor and replaces it on the sofa.*)

HILDEGARDE. But, Julia! If Mr. Thornton doesn't get a chance to see you alone, how can he ——?

JULIA. Oh, my goodness! How can he what?

HILDEGARDE. (*Solemnly*) Make you an offer. (*Ecstatically.*) Oh, he's so handsome!

JULIA. Oh, my goodness, Hildegarde, if you don't stop ——

HILDEGARDE. No woman could resist such a beautiful man. And oh—his neckties!

JULIA. (*Amused*) You take him then, Hildegarde! You're welcome to him! (*The door-bell rings.* JULIA *jumps up, clasps her hands together, doesn't know which way to run.*) Oh, dear! (*She looks in the mirror over the mantelpiece.*) I'm a fright! Where's my vanity? Oh—upstairs —— You let him in, Hildegarde! (*She rushes out.*)

HILDEGARDE. Don't go, Julia! You ought to be here when he comes in, Julia! Julia! Oh, *dear* ——! (*She starts for the door, returns, tiptoes to the mirror and fusses up her hair, starts again for the door, observes the cushion in place on the sofa. She tosses it down, leaves it, comes back, straightens it a little, pats it. The bell rings again. She hurries to the door.*)

THORNTON. (*Off stage*) Good-evening, Hildegarde.

HILDEGARDE. Why, good-evening, Mr. Thornton! How *do* you do? Please step right in and remove your coat. Let me hang it up for you. Cold night, isn't it? You want to see sister Julia, I suppose? I think she will receive you. Do come over here, please. (*With an elegant wave of the hand toward the sofa.*) Please be seated.

THORNTON. (*Sitting down.* HILDEGARDE *always amuses him*) You're looking mighty fit this evening, Shirley Temple. (*As he stretches his legs slightly, his feet touch the cushion on the floor.*)

HILDEGARDE. Oh, don't!
THORNTON. (*Startled*) What?
HILDEGARDE. You mustn't put your feet on that!
THORNTON. (*Embarrassed, examining his shoes*) Why—e—er ——
HILDEGARDE. It's not there for shoes.
THORNTON. Oh, I beg pardon! I thought it was a sort of a footstool. (*He stoops to pick it up.*)
HILDEGARDE. (*Restraining him*) No! I put it there, you see, for—for knees. (*He is puzzled. She interprets that as love's diffidence, and clasps her hands. Then she moves deliberately, with what she thinks is enormous dignity, to the door, and calls.*) Oh, sister Julia! Mr. Thornton is here.
JULIA. (*Off stage*) Be right down.

(*Meanwhile* THORNTON *has regarded his knees curiously, then the cushion, then his knees again. He can make nothing of* HILDEGARDE'S *remark. Now she returns.*)

THORNTON. You said knees. Is it some new kind of praying cushion?
HILDEGARDE. (*Beaming*) Yes. That's just what it is! A praying cushion. Gentlemen always kneel when they pray the fair lady of their heart ——
JULIA. (*Still off stage*) Hilde-garde! Come here a minute!
HILDEGARDE. (*Departing*) Gentlemen always kneel when they pray the fair lady of their heart to ——
[*She goes.*

(THORNTON'S *bewilderment gradually gives way to amusement. He chuckles, looks at the cushion, at his knees, chuckles again.*)

THORNTON. (*Speculatively*) I wonder if that kid meant me?

*THE WEDDING PRESENT
(Scene 1)

BY WILLIAM CARSON

SCENE.—*The living-room of the* GORDONS' *little suburban home.*

CHARACTERS: BOB GORDON.
CARRIE GORDON.

(BOB *and* CARRIE *have just returned from their honeymoon. Through some unexplainable circumstance the list of wedding gifts has been lost, or misplaced, and at the moment they are frantically engaged in trying to remember the gift of the friend who is to be their first dinner guest.* BOB *holds up a beautiful little Corot print.*)

CARRIE. (*Rapturously*) Oh, that lovely thing! Let me see it again. (*Taking it from him, she admires it.*) Do you know, I think that's quite the nicest present we've got.

BOB. And we don't know who sent it.

CARRIE. (*With sudden conviction and delight*) Bobbie! I do know! The mystery is solved. He sent it.

BOB. Who?

CARRIE. Who, stupid? Why, Jim Dixon, of course.

BOB. (*Incredulous*) Jim—sent that? Aw!

CARRIE. Why not?

BOB. Come off! You don't know him!

CARRIE. I've always heard he was artistic—went to the art museum and concerts, and wore artistic neckties.

BOB. Huh! He may be, but I never noticed it.

CARRIE. (*Sweetly*) Perhaps you wouldn't, dearest.

BOB. I know he'd never pick out anything like that. That's not the sort of picture he likes.

CARRIE. It's perfectly exquisite.

* Copyright, 1925, William Carson

Bob. May *be*. But that doesn't prove anything. He'd want something with lots of color—something to do with food probably. Say, there aren't any pictures of fruit or dead ducks hanging by their necks in the collection, are there?

Carrie. No, but there's one of a horse looking out of a stable-door.

Bob. He doesn't like horse-meat—lived in restaurants too much. (*During these remarks* Carrie *is inspecting one thing after another, moving objects about, stopping now and then to concentrate and then passing on to something else.* Bob, *with a sudden inspiration.*) My gosh, I've got it!

Carrie. What?

Bob. I know what he gave us.

Carrie. Thank Heaven! What?

Bob. Why didn't I think of it before? I *am* dumb!

Carrie. For goodness sake, then, what is it?

Bob. (*Transfixing her with a triumphant stare*) What a couple of ninnies we are! Of course, he gave us the electric roaster!

Carrie. (*Sinking into a chair*) Oh!

Bob. Well, what's the matter?

Carrie. How perfectly absurd!

Bob. I don't see why. I think the electric roaster is a very good thing.

Carrie. Of course it is. But *he* wouldn't give us *that*.

Bob. I don't see why not. A very sensible present.

Carrie. Yes, but not a thing he'd give us. It wouldn't be just exactly delicate.

Bob. Delicate or not, it's the kind of thing he's interested in. Anything related to food——

Carrie. Oh, stop it. He didn't give it to us. I've heard enough about him to know he's got too much taste.

Bob. (*Stubbornly*) I think it shows very good taste.

Carrie. He gave us the Corot.

Bob. He didn't.

Carrie. I beg your pardon.

Bob. I'm sorry. But I know Jim Dixon, and you don't. He gave us the roaster.

Carrie. The Corot.

Bob. (*Sarcastically*) Well, I'm glad we're agreed on that point.

Carrie. (*Putting the Corot in a conspicuous place*) I'm going to thank him for the picture.

Bob. (*Trying hard to be pleasant*) Good,—and I'll thank him for the roaster, just for fun, and see which of us hits the nail on the head.

Carrie. (*Disturbed*) You can't do that. We can't thank him for different things. What would he think of us?

Bob. What do you propose to do?

Carrie. (*Promptly*) Thank him for the Corot.

Bob. Oh, James, thanks so much for the dear—(*pauses for effect*)—roaster!

Carrie. (*Beginning to sniff*) I think you're horrid.

Bob. (*Embracing her*) Aw, come on! Let's not squabble over it. The darn thing isn't worth it. And he isn't, either.

Carrie. Then you'll thank him for the Corot?

Bob. I can't—because I *know* he didn't buy it.

Carrie. And I know he did. I don't see how you can be so stubborn. (*She sinks on chair or divan with that " I give it up " air.* Bob *walks about aimlessly, whistling to keep up his moral courage. Suddenly he stops, his mouth still in a pucker.* Carrie, *watching him, says suddenly* . . .) What in the world is the matter with you? Have you just eaten a sour pickle? *He turns to look at her, but still without restoring his lips to normalcy.*) BOB!

Bob. I just thought of a way to settle it.

Carrie. What is it?

Bob. We'll let him tell us himself.

Carrie. Do you mean we'll *ask* him? We'll do nothing of the sort.

Bob. No, we won't ask him. He won't know that he's telling us. (*She looks at him as if she feared he has taken leave of his senses.*) It's just this way. My scheme's all based on human nature—a fundamental weakness in human nature. You see it's like this: whenever anybody buys anything and gives it away, he, if he's paid real money for it,—he can't help having sort of subconscious regrets. He may not know it, but he has 'em. Now then, whenever he sees the things he's paid for and given away, he has an uncontrollable impulse to feel it—to fondle it. He mightn't do it if anybody was watching, but if he was left alone he couldn't help himself—he simply couldn't help himself. So you see what we've got to do.—When Jim comes, greet him politely, then just fade away, leaving him with all the presents about him. Then in a minute we'll pop in again, and presto,—the riddle is solved.

CARRIE. Did you think that all out yourself, Bobbie?

THE WEDDING PRESENT
(Scene 2)

BY WILLIAM CARSON

SCENE.—*A little while later. The guest has arrived and the usual greetings have been exchanged.*

CHARACTERS: CARRIE GORDON.
BOB GORDON.
JIM DIXON.

CARRIE. (*Rising hurriedly*) Dear me, I quite forgot the supper. I know you'll excuse me a few minutes, Jim.

JIM. (*Also rising*) Of course, certainly.

(CARRIE *goes to door, then stops a moment.*)

CARRIE. And I'm afraid I'll have to borrow my husband for a minute. Can you entertain yourself for a bit?

JIM. Yes,—by all means. (*He appears to be pleased.*)

(CARRIE *goes out and* BOB *follows her, but hesitates momentarily.*)

BOB. Just make yourself at home, old man. Take a

look about the room—and see what you think of things. (*Waves his hand airily to include everything and goes out.*)

(*As soon as he is alone,* JIM *hurries to the telephone and very cautiously, keeping his eyes on the doorway, dials a number. Waits nervously.*)

JIM. Hello......Hello......Is that you, Kate?...... I'm sorry......Isn't this Park 2656J? (*A little louder.*) What? I'm sorry......What did you say?......Oh, it *is* you, Kate! This is Jim......No, your *brother* Jim. ......I can't speak any louder. Say, I'm out at the Gordons' and I feel like a fool......Wha-a-a-a-t?...... I say I feel like a fool......Well, never mind what I said. Tell me what it was you got for me to give them for a wedding present......I *can't* speak any louder. ......What did you send them? I know it cost plenty, but what *was* it? I know you told me but I forgot. A what? (BOB *looks cautiously into the room and* JIM *drops the telephone but does not drop it into its proper position.* BOB *disappears and* JIM *hastily picks up the telephone.*) Hello......Kate......Hello, hello!...... Damnation!!

Complete copies of the plays from which these scenes are made can be supplied by the publishers

Tempo and Climax

Every play should have a distinctive tempo, or rate of movement, determined by the theme and mood of the story. This is accomplished by the speed of the spoken lines, the number and type of pauses, the picking up of cues, and the timing of the business.

In general, comedy should be played quickly, and meditative, contemplative moments more slowly. Rapid scenes, however, must not be so fast as to be unintelligible, and slower scenes must never drag. Very often tragedy moves swiftly, though quietly, and a brisk farce may have pauses.

In a full-length play there will be many changes in pace, this pulling-up and letting-down resulting in a rhythmic pattern which gives contrast and variety.

Throughout a play there will be moments of increased emotional intensity, or climaxes, which must be built up. This may be done in several ways, by accelerating the pace and increasing the volume as in quarrel scenes, or by suddenly decreasing the speed and volume when the emotion is suppressed and controlled. Some of the most moving climaxes are made by complete silence, or a simple expressive gesture.

In the following units, try to discover and develop a specific and appropriate tempo.

*WHAT MEN LIVE BY

(Scene 1)

From an Adaptation of the Story by Leo Tolstoi

BY VIRGINIA CHURCH

SCENE.—*A basement, reached by a few steps at the back leading to the outer door. Occasionally one sees the feet of pedestrians pass by the little window of the basement.*

CHARACTERS: SIMON, *the cobbler.*
MATRENA, *his wife.*

(SIMON, *old, slow in movement, kindly of feature, is seated at his cobbler's bench, mending a pair of shoes.* MATRENA *is seated on a stool, mending a tattered coat. This scene is offered as an example of contrast in tempo between two characters—*MATRENA, *quick;* SIMON, *slow.*)

MATRENA. And who was that went by, Simon?

SIMON. It was Thedka, my dear Matrena. Thedka, the footman of the Barina. The side-patch on his boot has lasted well.

MATRENA. Yes, you make them last for so long that they do not need to come to you and so you have little trade.

SIMON. But, Matrena, I could not put on patches that would not last; then I should have no trade at all. I must do my best. That is the kind of man I am.

MATRENA. Yes, yes, Simon, that is the kind of man you are and so this is the kind of home we have, with hardly enough flour in the bin for one baking.

* Copyright, 1924, Atlantic Monthly Press, Inc.

Simon. Don't fret, Matrena. We shall not starve. God is good.

Matrena. Aye, God is good, but His handmen are far from the likeness in which He cast them. (*A girl trips by.*) Was that Rozinka went by?

Simon. No, Rozinka has not such high heels. It was Ulka, the Barina's maid.

Matrena. I might have guessed it, after Thedka had passed. The minx is as hard on his footsteps as a man's shadow on a sunny day. It's a pity, since you shoe all the servants in the Baron's household, that the master would not let you make boots for him.

Simon. The boots of the nobilities are brought from Paris, and are cut from northern leather. Trofinoff told me he brought five pair from the station on his last trip.

Matrena. Trofinoff, h'm! Did you not tell me Trofinoff promised to come this afternoon to pay the eight roubles he has owed you three years coming Michaelmas?

Simon. Aye, so he said.

Matrena. So he said, but I'll warrant we never see a hair of his beard till he's come barefoot again. Now (*holding up the coat she is mending*) I've done all I can to your sheepskin. It's so thin the cold doesn't have to seek the holes to creep in; it walks through. It's thankful I'll be when we can buy another skin so that I can get out of the house the same time you go.

Simon. We'll buy a skin this very afternoon, my dear. When Trofinoff brings me the eight roubles, we shall add it to the three you have saved, and that ought to buy a good skin—if not a tanned one, at all events, a good rough one.

Matrena. *If* Trofinoff brings the money.

Simon. He'll bring it, or, by Heaven, I'll have the cap off his head, so I will. That is the kind of man I am.

Matrena. If he were to come in and tell you he is hard up, you would tell him not to worry his head about the roubles, that God is good.

Simon. No, I shall say, "Am I not hard up as well?"

Matrena. Very well, if he comes we shall see what kind of man you are. Who was that?

SIMON. It was your friend, Anna Maloska, who wears shoes too small for her.

MATRENA. She wore large shoes after she caught her husband; but now he is dead, she wears small shoes again to catch another.

SIMON. I wonder that she did not stop.

MATRENA. She will stop on her way back from market for there will be more news.

SIMON. (*Looking out the window and rising happily*) But see here, Matrena, you wronged the good Trofinoff. He has come to pay the eight roubles, as he promised. (*There is a halting knock at the door.*) Coming! Coming! (*He limps slightly as he hastens up the steps.*)

MATRENA. (*As she crosses to go into the room at* R.) Well, Simon, I shall be the last to be sorry if your faith has been rewarded. (*She goes out as* SIMON *opens the door to the street.*)

*RIDERS TO THE SEA

BY J. M. SYNGE

SCENE.—*An island off the west of Ireland. A cottage kitchen, with nets, oil-skins, spinning wheel, some new boards standing by the wall, etc.*

CHARACTERS: MAURYA, *an old woman.*
BARTLEY, *her son.*
CATHLEEN, *her daughter.*
NORA, *a younger daughter.*

(CATHLEEN, *a girl of about twenty, finishes kneading cake and puts it down in the pot-oven by the fire; then wipes her hands and begins to spin at the wheel.* NORA, *a young girl, puts her head in at the door, then comes in softly, and takes a bundle from under her shawl.*)

* Copyright, 1916, by L. E. Bassett

CATHLEEN. (*Spinning the wheel rapidly*) What is it you have?

NORA. The young priest is after bringing them. It's a shirt and a plain stocking were got off a drowned man in Donegal. (CATHLEEN *stops her wheel with a sudden movement, and leans out to listen.*) We're to find out if it's Michael's they are, some time herself will be down looking by the sea.

CATHLEEN. How would they be Michael's, Nora? How would he go the length of that way to the far north?

NORA. The young priest says he's known the like of it.

(*The door which* NORA *half closed is blown open by a gust of wind.*)

CATHLEEN. (*Looking out anxiously*) Did you ask him would he stop Bartley going this day with the horses to the Galway fair?

NORA. "I won't stop him," says he, "but let you not be afraid. Herself does be saying prayers half through the night, and the Almighty God won't leave her destitute," says he, "with no son living."

CATHLEEN. Is the sea bad by the white rocks, Nora?

NORA. Middling bad, God help us. There's a great roaring in the west, and it's worse it'll be getting when the tide's turned to the wind. (*She goes over to the table with the bundle.*) Shall I open it now?

CATHLEEN. Maybe she'd wake up on us, and come in before we'd done. (*Coming to the table.*) It's a long time we'll be, and the two of us crying.

NORA. (*Goes to the inner door and listens*) She's moving about on the bed. She'll be coming in a minute.

CATHLEEN. I'll put them in the turf-loft, the way she won't know of them at all, and maybe when the tide turns she'll be going down to see would he be floating from the east. (*She goes to chimney-corner and hides the bundle.*)

(MAURYA *comes from the inner room.*)

MAURYA. (*Looking up at* CATHLEEN *and speaking*

querulously) Isn't it turf enough you have for this day and evening?

CATHLEEN. There's a cake baking at the fire for a short space, (*throwing down the turf*) and Bartley will want it when the tide turns if he goes to Connemara.

(NORA *picks up the turf and puts it round the pot-oven.*)

MAURYA. (*Sitting down on a stool at the fire*) He won't go this day with the wind rising from the south and west. He won't go this day, for the young priest will stop him surely.

NORA. He'll not stop him, mother.

MAURYA. Where is he itself?

NORA. He went down to see would there be another boat sailing in the week, and I'm thinking it won't be long till he's here now, for the tide's turning at the green head, and the hooker's tacking from the east.

CATHLEEN. I hear someone passing the big stones.

NORA. (*Looking out*) He's coming now, and he in a hurry.

BARTLEY. (*Comes in and looks round the room. Speaking sadly and quietly*) Where is the bit of new rope, Cathleen, was bought in Connemara?

CATHLEEN. (*Coming down*) Give it to him, Nora; it's on a nail by the white boards. I hung it up this morning, for the pig with the black feet was eating it.

NORA. (*Giving him a rope*) Is that it, Bartley?

MAURYA. You'd do right to leave that rope, Bartley, hanging by the boards. (BARTLEY *takes the rope.*) It will be wanting in this place, I'm telling you, if Michael is washed up tomorrow morning, or the next morning, or any morning in the week, for it's a deep grave we'll make him by the grace of God.

BARTLEY. (*Beginning to work with the rope*) I've no halter the way I can ride down on the mare, and I must go now quickly. This is the one boat going for two weeks or beyond it, and the fair will be a good fair for horses I heard them saying below.

MAURYA. It's a hard thing they'll be saying below if

the body is washed up and there's no man in it to make the coffin, and I after giving a price for the finest white boards you'd find in Connemara. (*She looks round at the boards.*)

BARTLEY. How would it be washed up, and after looking each day for nine days, and a strong wind blowing a while back from the west and south?

MAURYA. If it wasn't found itself, that wind is raising the sea, and there was a star up against the moon, and it rising in the night. If it was a hundred horses, or a thousand horses you had itself, what is the price of a thousand horses against a son where there is one son only?

BARTLEY. (*Working at the halter, to* CATHLEEN) Let you go down each day, and see the sheep aren't jumping in on the rye, and if the jobber comes you can sell the pig with the black feet if there is a good price going.

MAURYA. How would the like of her get a good price for a pig?

BARTLEY. (*To* CATHLEEN) If the west wind holds with the last bit of the moon let you and Nora get up weed enough for another cock for the kelp. It's hard set we'll be from this day with no one in it but one man to work.

MAURYA. It's hard set we'll be surely the day you're drownd'd with the rest. What way will I live and the girls with me, and I an old woman looking for the grave?

BARTLEY. (*Laying down the halter, takes off his old coat and puts on a newer one of the same flannel. Speaks to* NORA.) Is she coming to the pier?

NORA. (*Looking out*) She's passing the green head and letting fall her sails.

BARTLEY. (*Getting his purse and tobacco*) I'll have half an hour to go down, and you'll see me coming again in two days, or in three days, or maybe in four days if the wind is bad.

MAURYA. (*Turning round to the fire, and putting her shawl over her head*) Isn't it a hard and cruel man won't hear a word from an old woman, and she holding him from the sea?

CATHLEEN. It's the life of a young man to be going on

the sea, and who would listen to an old woman with one thing and she saying it over?

BARTLEY. (*Taking the halter*) I must go now quickly. I'll ride down on the red mare, and the gray pony'll run behind me. . . . The blessing of God on you.

[*He goes out.*

MAURYA. (*Crying out as he is in the door*) He's gone now, God spare us, and we'll not see him again. He's gone now, and when the black night is falling I'll have no son left me in the world.

*THE AFFAIRS OF MEN

(Scene 2)

BY WARREN BECK

SCENE.—*A waiting room in a railway station in Chicago.*

CHARACTERS: THE NEW YORK BOY.
THE SAN FRANCISCO BOY.

(*The boys have struck up an acquaintance while waiting for their respective trains. The conversation has been amiable up to this point.*)

NEW YORK. 'Frisco, you haven't seen anything yet! Wait until you see New York! There's only one New York, you know!

SAN FRANCISCO. Maybe so. But where are you on climate? Don't forget the California climate. Sunshine and flowers the year around. None of your blizzards—no ice and snow and zero weather.

NEW YORK. We don't mind that. Why, we like our winters. You ought to see the lights of Broadway at night in a snowstorm. It's prettier than all your California flowers.

* Copyright, 1931, Walter H. Baker Company

San Francisco. Well, it's a comfortable place, California is.

New York. So's New York. And things happen in New York.

San Francisco. Believe me, things happen in 'Frisco, too.

New York. Oh, I suppose people die there. At that you can't blame 'em.

San Francisco. Say, I'd rather die in 'Frisco than live in New York.

New York. Then why didn't you stay out there with your Chink cooks?

San Francisco. Why didn't you stay in New York, if you think it's so great? If there's two men for every job, you still have that big harbor—you can always go jump in that.

New York. You jumping-jack elevator boy, are you trying to get funny with me? (*Getting up, approaching opponent.*)

San Francisco. Suppose I am, you skillet-scrubber, what are you going to do about it? There ain't no meat axes around here for you to fight with.

New York. (*Looking past* San Francisco) Ssst! A cop! (*Sits down.*)

San Francisco. (*Looking over his shoulder, verifying fact, sits down*) Did he see us?

New York. (*In an acrimonious whisper*) No, but it's a wonder he didn't hear you.

San Francisco. Hear me? Say, you made more noise than I did—you ——

New York. (*Voice rising*) *I* made more noise than you did? Why, you brass-buttoned —— (*He is searching for an epithet.*)

San Francisco. Listen to you now, you loud-mouthed potato peeler. You ——

New York. Yeah! (*He forces himself to lower his voice but not his vehemence.*) You been riding an elevator cage so long that you're crazy. Eating Chink cooking, too—that's made you crazy, too. Been eating rats, I suppose.

San Francisco. I've been living on better food and

cleaner food in 'Frisco than you ever saw in your dirty New York hash house.

NEW YORK. Dirty? Say, they're particular where I worked!

SAN FRANCISCO. They couldn't be if they let you in the kitchen.

NEW YORK. (*Jumping up*) You monkey-faced door-opener, I'll knock you back where you came from!

SAN FRANCISCO. (*Jumping up and making a belligerent approach*) Come on—just start it once! (*Changing tone suddenly.*) Sssst! Lay off. The cop's coming back.

NEW YORK. (*Taking a glance*) He's standing back there. (*They sit down.*) You'll be getting us in trouble in a minute.

SAN FRANCISCO. *I* will? Say, whose fault is this? Who started this?

NEW YORK. You're not insinuating I started it?

SAN FRANCISCO. Well, what did I do?

NEW YORK. You shouldn't have got insulting.

SAN FRANCISCO. You started the insults.

NEW YORK. I did not.

SAN FRANCISCO. Well, you said plenty.

NEW YORK. Oh, yeah! You said your share, too.

SAN FRANCISCO. Well—maybe I did.

NEW YORK. Well—at that—I guess we've both got a grouch on.

SAN FRANCISCO. Yeh, that's it; I guess you're right.

(NEW YORK *takes a cigarette, puts it into his mouth, then offers the package to* SAN FRANCISCO, *who accepts in silence. He supplies* NEW YORK *with a light before lighting his own cigarette.*)

*CATHERINE PARR

by Maurice Baring

SCENE.—*London. Breakfast chamber in the Palace.*

Characters: KING HENRY VIII.
CATHERINE PARR.

(King Henry *and* Catherine *are discovered sitting opposite to each other at the breakfast table. The king has just cracked a boiled egg.*)

King Henry. My egg's raw. It really is too bad.

Catherine. Yesterday you complained of their being hard.

King Henry. And so they were. I don't want a hard egg, and I don't want a raw egg. I want them to be cooked just right.

Catherine. You are very difficult to please. The egg was in boiling water for three minutes and a half. I boiled it myself. But give it to me. I like them like that. I will boil you another.

King Henry. No. It's too late now. But it is a fact that you have no idea how to boil an egg. I wish you'd let them do them in the kitchen.

Catherine. If they're done in the kitchen you complain because they're not here when you come down, and if they are here, you say they're cold.

King Henry. I never say anything of the kind. The cook boils eggs beautifully.

Catherine. She shall boil them tomorrow.

King Henry. One would have thought that a woman of your experience might at least know how to boil an egg. I hate a watery egg. (*Pensively.*) Poor, dear Katie used to boil eggs beautifully.

Catherine. Do you mean Catherine Howard or Katherine of Aragon?

* Copyright, 1928, Walter H Baker Company

KING HENRY. I was alluding to poor, dear, misguided Katie Howard. Katherine of Aragon never was my wife. The marriage was not valid.

CATHERINE. Well, Catherine Howard ought to have known how to boil eggs, considering her mother was a kitchenmaid.

KING HENRY. That is utterly untrue. Her mother was a Rockford.

CATHERINE. You're thinking of Anne Bullen.

KING HENRY. Yes, yes, to be sure. Katie's mother was a Somerset.

CATHERINE. You're thinking of Jane Seymour.

KING HENRY. Not at all. Jane Seymour was a sister of Somerset's.

CATHERINE. All I know is that Catherine Howard's mother was a kitchenmaid. And I think it's very unkind of you to mention her to me. I suppose you mean that you wish she were alive, and that you loved her better than you love me.

KING HENRY. I never said anything of the kind. All I said was that she knew how to boil eggs.

CATHERINE. You clearly meant to say that she had all the qualities which I lack.

KING HENRY. You are most unfair. I never meant to hint at any such thing. All I said was that I hate a watery egg, and my egg this morning was raw.

CATHERINE. (*Rising and going to the door in a temper*) Well, the best thing you can do is to get rid of me, and to marry someone who knows how to boil an egg.

KING HENRY. Catherine, come back! I really didn't mean to offend you. You know how to boil eggs very well.

CATHERINE. One takes an endless amount of trouble, and that's all the thanks one gets. Don't think I shall ever boil your eggs for you again, because I shan't! (*Dashes angrily from the room, leaving* KING HENRY *greatly perturbed.*)

*THE SHORT CUT

by Percival Wilde

SCENE.—*A darkness so complete that nothing whatever is visible through it.*

CHARACTERS: BOB.
STEVE.

(*There is silence. Presently there is a sound of slow, rhythmical tapping of a hammer on stone: clink, clink, clink,—clink, clink, clink —— A pause. Then the tapping is resumed. Slowly, regularly, it taps out its message. It stops.*)

STEVE. (*A harsh, grating voice; the voice of a man on the verge of a breakdown*) Bob!
BOB. (*A much calmer voice*) Well?
STEVE. Bob, how long do you reckon we've been here now?
BOB. Two days.
STEVE. Two days? Then it's Thursday.
BOB. Wednesday.
STEVE. Wednesday? That all?
BOB. I don't think it's any longer than that. It was Monday afternoon when the roof caved in behind us.
STEVE. Yes. Yes! It was Monday! Two days ago! That's why today's Wednesday. Yes. It *is* Wednesday. You're right. You're always right. (*He laughs hysterically. The tapping of the hammer commences. He stops laughing abruptly.*) Do you think they'll hear that?
BOB. My hammer?
STEVE. Yes, your hammer.
BOB. Maybe they will.
STEVE. (*With derision*) Maybe they won't!
BOB. Maybe they won't. (*The tapping recommences.*)

* Copyright, 1931, Percival Wilde

STEVE. Maybe they won't. Then we'll stay here—Wednesday—until a week from Wednesday—until a year from Wednesday! We'll stay here and die—slowly—slowly —— (*Silence, except for the sound of the hammer.*) Once—once I knew a chap who used to carry a tablet of poison. (*He pauses.*)

BOB. Yes? (*The tapping stops.*)

STEVE. He never went down a shaft without his tablet. He said that if he were ever caught—the way we're caught now—he wouldn't wait to starve to death. No, not he! He wouldn't wait for the rats to start eating him before the breath was out of his body. He'd take a short cut. Whatever happened, he'd cheat the rats.

BOB. (*After a pause*) Wise man, your friend. (*The tapping recommences.*)

STEVE. (*Semi-hysterically*) Wasn't he? Wasn't he? I'll say he was!

BOB. You—you don't happen to have some of his poison with you?

STEVE. What do you want with it?

BOB. If the worst comes to the worst—it might come in handy.

STEVE. (*Laughing loudly*) Well, I haven't got any! No such luck! (*A pause; the sound of the hammer, which has ceased, begins again. Suddenly.*) Stop it! Stop it, I say!

BOB. What?

STEVE. It drives me crazy!

BOB. Steve!

STEVE. I tell you that hammering of yours is driving me crazy! Stop it!

BOB. It's our only chance, Steve.

STEVE. I don't care if it is—and I don't believe it is. Stop it! (*The tapping stops.*) It's bad enough to be caught in this miserable trap! It's bad enough to know we've got to sit here till we die of starvation! It's bad enough to wait—wait—wait—without you ticking the seconds away so that I can't forget them as they go by!

BOB. (*After a pause*) Steve, I don't like to starve any more than you do.

STEVE. (*Harshly, hysterically*) Do you think I care

whether you like it or not? I haven't had a bite to eat in two days. I'm not thinking of you at a time like this!

Bob. (*Gently*) All right, Steve. . . . I'm going to start hammering again.

Steve. Don't.

Bob. They may hear it.

Steve. They? They? Overhead? Quarter of a mile above us, in God's good air and sunshine? Why, they haven't missed us yet.

Bob. I told you I heard the sound of a pick.

Steve. Yes: when a man's beginning to starve, he hears things.

Bob. They're down in the mine by now. They're hunting for us. You can depend on that. (*He resumes tapping.*)

Steve. (*After a pause*) A lot of good it'll do! . . . Ten—twenty miles of drifts and crosscuts—and three-quarters of them choked up with rock falls! They've got no chance of finding us. Why, it would take a hundred men a year to explore the mine!

Bob. But I heard the sound of a pick.

Steve. You'll hear funnier things than that—before the end. You'll hear the rats—coming closer than they dare now. You'll hear voices—when you know there can't be any voices. It's an old mine, and it's working all the time; and you'll hear anything you want to hear. You'll hear music—and waterfalls—and birds singing—and ——

Bob. (*Interrupting*) Shut up, Steve. (*There is a long pause, during which is heard only the sound of the tapping.*)

Steve. Got another cigarette?

Bob. Here, take it.

Steve. Light?

Bob. Here.

(*A patent lighter flares, revealing for an instant the interior of a tiny cave in which two men, dressed in the rough clothing of mining engineers, are sitting. The lighter is extinguished. Darkness returns, seemingly blacker than before. Through it we see the glimmer of the burning cigarette.*)

STEVE. Lord, that's good. (*He pauses.*) You're not smoking, Bob.
BOB. No.
STEVE. Why not?
BOB. That was my last cigarette. (*The tapping recommences.*)
STEVE. (*Incredulously*) Honest? (*There is no reply. He becomes bitter.*) You were always generous, weren't you? You were like that back in our college days,—eh? (*There is no answer except the sound of the hammer. . . .*)

*WHEN THE SUN RISES

BY DOROTHY C. ALLAN

SCENE.—*A living-room. In the* R. *wall are two doors; in the* L. *wall a French window. A davenport is placed down* C., *and in the corner, up* L., *is a telephone on a small stand.*

CHARACTERS: THE NURSE.
LOUISE.
TOM.

(*The curtain rises to the insistent ringing of the telephone. From* U. R. *door a nurse enters and, crossing to the telephone, speaks in a hushed tone.*)

NURSE. Miss Manton speaking......Oh, yes, Dr. Ware......Yes, just as you directed......Not yet. He regains consciousness for a few minutes at a time, only to slip off again. Yes, very restless......No, I think not. ......The girl? Just as you left her. She's breathing,

* Copyright, 1933, Fitzgerald Publishing Corporation

but that's all. I think there's quite a doubt whether——
......I see......Yes, I will......Miss Price is lying down. I persuaded her to get some rest......Oh, of course, a great shock to her. Not many people would have taken in two perfect strangers, but she's always so——......Yes, certainly. I'll notify you of any change. Good-bye. [*Goes off* D. R.

(*Almost at once,* LOUISE *enters* U. R. *She is in evening dress and enters in a furtive, bewildered fashion, looking back as if afraid of being followed. She advances to* C., *with a long shuddering sigh raises both arms as if to brush away a veil of mist, looks around the room, crosses to the French window, looks out, then turns away, returns to* C. *and begins calling in a low voice.*)

LOUISE. Tom! Tom! Where are you? (*She sits cautiously on the davenport with timid glances around as if expecting the presence of an unseen danger.*) He must come! He must come!—Tom! Oh, where are you? (*A low murmur comes from the door* D. R. *She starts toward it.*) Tom, dear, are you there? Here I am—out here. Come to me. Quick!

(*Through the door* D. R. *comes a young man in evening attire. He holds his hand to his forehead dazedly.*)

TOM. Someone call me? That you, Louise? Where are you?
LOUISE. (*Hurrying to him*) Oh, Tom, I'm so glad. I was afraid you'd left me, and it's terrifying—going alone.

(*Mechanically he puts an arm around her and in a sort of stupor lets her lead him to the davenport. His voice is at first hollow and expressionless.*)

TOM. Left you? Left you where? What's the idea? Whew! I'm sleepy. (*Sinks down on davenport and leans his head back.*)

LOUISE. No, no, you mustn't be! Not now. Wake up, darling. It's our only hope of staying together. Wake up! (*Shakes him frantically.*) Listen to me, Tom. Can you hear me? Can you see me?

TOM. (*Drowsily*) Of course I can hear you, and I could see you if I could keep my eyes open long enough.

LOUISE. Oh, try, Tom! Try as you've never tried anything before. You must! Look at me!

(*With an effort he brushes his hand across his eyes and looks at her. He straightens his shoulders and his face becomes alert, his voice clear and strong.*)

TOM. Well, you certainly are worth looking at.

LOUISE. (*Sinks back against the cushions and laughs hysterically*) Oh, thank goodness—thank goodness you've come. It's been awful! I thought you'd never get through to me. I've tried and tried and I kept getting more and more frightened.

TOM. Frightened? Of what?

LOUISE. Of going alone. But now that you're here, it's all right.

TOM. It can't be time to go home yet, and you wouldn't go alone, anyhow. Silly of me to fall asleep, though—didn't know I was so tired. (*He rises.*) We'd better get back to the ballroom—mustn't miss the last dance. By the way, why's the music stopped? And—I don't remember coming into this room. I must have been mighty tired. Come along, dear.

(LOUISE *has risen and is looking at him fixedly.*)

LOUISE. The last dance? The music? But, Tom, don't you remember,—don't you know ——?

TOM. Know what? (*He laughs as he puts his arm around her.*) Was it being serious again? That's no way to behave at a party. Worse than going to sleep. Let's run along now before the others miss us.

LOUISE. Tom, sit down. (*She sits, and pulls him down beside her.*) You've got to get this straight before we start out. Think—what happened last night?

Tom. Last night? Nothing. I sat home and read a dumb book and thought about you.

Louise. No, no! That was the night before. I mean last night. The dance.

Tom. Honey, you didn't drink too much of that punch, did you? Last night, she says, when the dance is right now.

Louise. (*Impatiently*) Do you hear music? Do you see anything around you that looks like Joan's house?

Tom. Well, no, but ——

Louise. (*Rising and leading him to the window*) Come here. Look. What do you see out there?

Tom. Not much. It's too dark. There's just a streak of light down at the horizon. Say! The rain must have stopped. We can drive home all right. Can't say I relish driving on wet roads.

Louise. Dawn is just breaking. Look off there toward the left.

Tom. Looks like a dark hump—a hill, perhaps.

Louise. A hill—a steep hill, Tom, with a sharp curve at the bottom.

Tom. (*Turning away and yawning*) Um! Interesting—but I was never very keen on geography. Do you know, I'm still sleepy!

Louise. Tom, think! A steep hill—beating rain—a country road slippery with mud—a sharp curve ——

(Tom *wheels quickly and stands for a minute, tense, hand to head.*)

Tom. (*Sharply*) Louise! Louise! (*She hurries to him.*) Am I dreaming—or remembering? It seems as if —— Wait a minute. It's all coming back. We were driving fast ——

Louise. Yes—yes ——

Tom. On that hill we skidded—I jammed on the brake—it wouldn't hold—we raced down—and at the bottom—at the curve ——

Louise. (*Putting her hand over his mouth*) Don't, darling, don't.

(*For a minute they cling together silently.*)

Tom. Great Godfrey! What a narrow escape! How could I have forgotten it even enough to sleep? Why, honey, that might have been our last ride.

Louise. Our last ride—yes.

Tom. (*Laughing shakily*) Well, a fool for luck! Maybe that'll teach me not to drive so fast.—But I don't remember coming here.

Louise. We were carried here. They must have heard the smash and found us.

Tom. That was pretty decent of someone. We'll have to thank them before we start on. Poor little girl! No wonder you were frightened after an experience like that. (*He feels himself thoughtfully.*) I don't feel bruised, do you? And your dress isn't even soiled or torn. I'd better go back and see about the car.

(Louise, *who has been again standing at the window, looking out, turns back to stop him with a hand on his arm.*)

Louise. Dear, we haven't much more time, and you've got to understand.

Tom. Understand what? I don't need to understand anything except that we both escaped getting smashed up. Why, we might even have been put out of commission for next Thursday—and it's bad luck to postpone a wedding.

Louise. (*Desperately*) Tom, listen! We *were* smashed up—so badly smashed that ——

Tom. Well?

Louise. When the sun rises ——

Tom. When the sun rises ——

Louise. We—we must —— (*Unable to go on, she points toward the two doors.*)

Tom. (*Puzzled, looks at her, then at the doors, finally crosses* R. *and looks first into one room, then the other. He comes back and stands quietly beside her. There is a trace of worry in his voice*) There's a fellow in the bed in one room—a girl in the other. I couldn't see their faces, but somehow they look ——

Louise. Yes.
Tom. Are they—dead?
Louise. When the sun rises ——

(*Slowly an expression of horror grows on his face. Another investigation of the rooms brings him back, pale with realization.*)

Tom. I see. Those two are—you and I.
Louise. You and I.
Tom. Then we are—dying?

(Louise, *looking up at his tense face, stretches out a hand to take his.*)

Complete copies of the plays from which these scenes are made can be supplied by the publishers

Radio Broadcasting

For those schools where a radio studio has been set up in the classroom and radio broadcasting instruction is offered, we conclude this hand-book with two scenes from radio adaptations. One is of a play which has proven its worth in production by school groups, namely, NOT QUITE SUCH A GOOSE. The other is an illustration of the popular manner of presenting radio dramatizations of standard works of literature, in this instance, THE GOLD BUG, by Edgar Allan Poe.

NOT QUITE SUCH A GOOSE

BY ELIZABETH GALE

Adapted for the Radio by Roger Wheeler

(*The scene of the action is laid in the well-worn living-room of the Bells on a summer day of the present.*)

CHARACTERS: MRS. BELL, *a happy mother.*
ALBERT BELL, *her 17-year-old son.*
SYLVIA BELL, *her daughter.*
PHILIP FLICK, *Sylvia's sweetheart.*

(*SOUND EFFECT. Door bangs open.*)

ALBERT. (*Voice fades in*) H'llo, Mom. Say, we trimmed 'em!

MRS. BELL. Good!

ALBERT. You should have seen me pitch those last two innings, Mom. They couldn't hit a ball. Say, I wish you'd come to a game sometime.

MRS. BELL. I am going to some day. Don't you think, dear, you'd better go and wash up?

ALBERT. Sure. But if you think I'm dirty, you ought to see Bud Mixie. He slid on his face halfway from the third base home.

MRS. BELL. (*Astonished*) He did! And he lives halfway down the turnpike.

ALBERT. Ha, ha. That's a good one. I mean *home* on the diamond.

MRS. BELL. Oh, I see. Wouldn't tennis be a nicer game to play?

ALBERT. *That* sissy game!! Never! Say, what are we having for dessert?

MRS. BELL. I promised you huckleberry pudding, didn't I?

ALBERT. I wanted to see if you remembered. All right, I'll go wash. (*Voice fades out whistling.*)

SYLVIA. (*In distance*) Oh, Mother. (*Voice fades*

in.) Ugh! I see Albert is home with all his baseball mess.

MOTHER. Now, Sylvia! Did you get all the errands?

SYLVIA. Yes, everything. And, oh, Mother, I met Hazel Henderson and asked her over to dinner. Is that all right?

MRS. BELL. Why, why I guess so. We'll only have huckleberry pudding for dessert, and ——

SYLVIA. Oh, not huckleberry pudding, Mother. It makes the mouth all black.

MRS. BELL. But I promised Albert.

SYLVIA. But, Mother, please just this once don't let Albert plan your meals for you. After supper Philip Flick is coming and—and ——

MRS. BELL. (*Understanding*) And black mouths are not becoming. I see.

SYLVIA. You know it looks perfectly horrid. And besides, we're going to the movies, if you don't mind.

MRS. BELL. That will be very nice.

SYLVIA. Philip was going to take me and—er—do you suppose you could coax Albert to take Hazel?

MRS. BELL. Not without the pudding. You know he's at the age when he despises girls anyway, and he particularly dislikes Hazel.

SYLVIA. Why, Mother, he doesn't know her. He hasn't seen her for four years. I have kept in touch with her while she's been away, but Albert wouldn't know her if he fell over her.

MRS. BELL. Well, I'll see what I can do. Of course I'd like him to go with her tonight, but you know how boys are. I've got to see about dinner, too, Sylvia. (*Voice fades out. In distance.*) Philip is coming through the garden now.

SYLVIA. Oh, Philip! Come in! Will you sit down?

PHILIP. No, thanks, I just dropped in to make sure it was all right about tonight.

SYLVIA. Perfectly all right. We'll be ready at seven.

PHILIP. *We?*

SYLVIA. Hazel Henderson is back home and she's coming here to supper, and then ——

PHILIP. And then to the movies with *us?*

Sylvia. I am going to get someone to go with her so there will be two couples—just a nice party.

Philip. Fine. Well, I'll be running. Er—that's a beautiful rose you're wearing.

Sylvia. I just picked it in the garden.

Philip. May I have it?

Sylvia. Of course, Philip. But there are nicer ones on the bush.

Philip. But I prefer this one. Will you pin it on me?

Sylvia. Gladly.

Philip. You know just how to do it, don't you?

Sylvia. I love to handle flowers.

Philip. I'm sure they love it, too. I feel that I belong to the Legion of Honor.

Sylvia. You belong to a smaller group than that. I don't give roses to everyone.

Philip. You darling! We're going to tell them soon, aren't we?

Sylvia. Very soon. You'd better leave now if you're going to get back by seven.

Philip. All right. Seven sharp. (*Voice fades out.*)

(*SOUND EFFECT. Door opens and shuts. Pause.*)

Albert. (*Voice fades in—affected and falsetto*) What a beautiful rose. Pin it on for me, dearie. No, I don't like those on the bush—they ain't good enough for me.

Sylvia. You mean, hateful boy! You were listening.

Albert. I couldn't help it. I stood right there in the doorway, but you and Philip were too lovey-dovey to see anything. Ah-h-h, what a rose.

Sylvia. You—you—villain.

Albert. If you call me names, I'll insist on the huckleberry pudding. I said I'd give it up if I wouldn't have to take old Hazel Nut to the movies tonight.

Sylvia. Pig!

Albert. Cow!

Sylvia. You're the meanest, nastiest thing in the whole world.

Albert. It runs in the family.

SYLVIA. Go finish dressing. Put on a tie and coat. You look like a freak.

ALBERT. (*Teasing*) I guess I'll stay this way.

SYLVIA. You're a nasty tease.

ALBERT. (*Mocking*) Philip de—ar. A rose for Philip. *Paroxysm of laughter.*)

SYLVIA. You mean thing. I'll—I'll shake you.

ALBERT. Murder! Help! Ha, ha, ha!

MRS. BELL. (*Voice fades in*) Children! Children!

SYLVIA. Mother, he is the meanest thing!

MRS. BELL. Sylvia, I'm ashamed of you!

SYLVIA. He started to ——

ALBERT. I did not. I never touched her, and she began to pummel me. I wonder what Philip would have said if he had seen ——

SYLVIA. I won't stay here. (*Voice fades out.*)

(*SOUND EFFECT. Door opens and slams shut.*)

MRS. BELL. I suppose you were teasing her again.

ALBERT. Aw, can't a fellow have any fun?

MRS. BELL. Not at somebody else's expense. I must say, Albert, you behave more like a child of seven than a young gentleman of seventeen.

ALBERT. If you could have seen them, Mom, you would have laughed yourself. (*Mocking.*) Oh, what a be-autiful rose. Oh, oh! Ha, ha, ha!

MRS. BELL. (*Quietly amused*) I suppose it was all very foolish to you.

ALBERT. They talked for half an hour about a dinky little rose. Ha, ha.

MRS. BELL. Of course, you'd never do anything so absurd.

ALBERT. I! Humph! I'm not quite such a goose.

MRS. BELL. But you are growing up, my son.

ALBERT. Say, Mom, would you like me to be like sissy Philip Flick?

MRS. BELL. No, dear. Just like your own dear self.

... You know, we are having a guest tonight, Albert. If you combed your hair and fixed up a little—it would please me very much.

ALBERT. All right, Mother. But I'm not going to take Hazel Nut anywhere. I gave up the pudding, you know ——

MRS. BELL. Yes, I know. Now be good until dinner. (*Voice fades out.*)

THE GOLD BUG

Dramatized and adapted for the radio from the works of Edgar Allan Poe

BY FREDERICK GARRIGUS

(*This is a scene from a half hour radio broadcast including musical selections and the dialogue of the announcer and* NARRATOR.)

CHARACTERS: NARRATOR. (*This should be the same for the entire series. He sets the scene of the play and relates biographical bits about Poe.*)
WILLIAM LEGRAND. (*A once wealthy Southern gentleman, now destitute and living with one servant on the desolate Sullivan's Island. This character is marked by the sudden flares of temper and the feverish enthusiasms of the chronic collector and hermit.*)
FRIENDLING. (*A close friend of Legrand's. A man of poise and balance. Cultured and well bred.*)
JUPITER. (*Negro servant of Legrand's. Speaks in a very pronounced Southern manner and is slow in speech and thought. He is very superstitious.*)

(*MUSICAL INTRODUCTION. Suitable theme music is played during the opening and closing announcements of each episode of this series, and during the dialogue of the* NARRATOR. *This music should be the same for each broadcast, and thus serve to identify this series. The music should commence forte and quickly change to diminuendo and so continue underneath the dialogue of the* ANNOUNCER *and the* NARRATOR.)

ANNOUNCER. At this time we present the first in a new series of Tales of Mystery and Adventure adapted for the radio from the life and works of Edgar Allan Poe. Mr. ———, the Narrator for this series, will set the scene of today's story and tell you something of how Poe came to write this thrilling story; Mr. ———.

NARRATOR. Thank you, Mr. ———. In the year 1809, the year in which Lincoln, Holmes, Tennyson, and Chopin were born, Eliza Arnold, the young actress-wife of David Poe, gave birth to a son whom they named Edgar. Henry Longfellow was a tottering infant of two years on that eventful winter's day when the unhappiest and most gifted writer America had ever produced was born in Boston. Something of the want and privation which was to dog the footsteps of Edgar Poe was to be seen in the privations and failures of his father and mother. After their death, Edgar was adopted into the home of Mr. John Allan, a well-to-do merchant of Richmond, from whom Edgar took his middle name of Allan. For our dramatization of one of Poe's tales of mystery and adventure today we offer *The Gold Bug*. It is interesting to note that *The Gold Bug* was first published in the Dollar Newspaper, as an entrant in a $100 prize writing contest. The scene of *The Gold Bug* is laid on Sullivan's Island, off the coast of Charleston, South Carolina. During the years 1827 and 1828, Poe had served, under an assumed name, in the United States Army, and had been stationed at Fort Moultrie—the very spot where he later laid the scene of *The Gold Bug*. In the inmost recesses of Sullivan's Island, William Legrand has built himself a small hut, where he and an old Negro servant, Jupiter, live in quiet retirement, enjoying themselves collecting shells and odd specimens of insects. Friendling, an old acquaintance of Legrand's, who is staying at Charleston, has called to visit the hermit on his lonely island, as today's story opens. It is an unusually chilly day in the month of October, and Friendling has built a rousing fire in the old shack. He sits warming himself while awaiting the return of Legrand and his servant, Jupiter, from one of their expeditions. It is nearly dark before footsteps on the gravel path announce the return of the hunters.

(*STOP THEME MUSIC. PAUSE. SOUND EFFECT. Door opens and closes in the distance.*)

LEGRAND. (*Conversation fades in*) I tell you, Jupiter, it's the greatest thing I've ever found!

JUPITER. Yes, sir, Massa Will, it sure am. It's a great little bug! Ah, here's Massa Friendling!

FRIENDLING. Well, Legrand, I began to think that I wasn't going to see you after all!

LEGRAND. Friendling, I'm glad you're here; I've discovered an entirely new genus of beetle today, and tomorrow I want to get your opinion on it!

FRIENDLING. Tomorrow? Why not tonight?

LEGRAND. Ah, if I had only known that you were here! But it's so long since I've seen you; and how could I know that you would pay me a visit this very night of all others?

FRIENDLING. How is tonight any different than any other in this forsaken place?

LEGRAND. Just wait until you hear what it is I've found! A new genus of beetle! As I was coming home I met a friend from the Fort, and, very foolishly, I lent it to him. Stay here tonight, and I'll send Jup down for it at sunrise. It is the loveliest thing in creation!

FRIENDLING. What—the sunrise?

LEGRAND. Nonsense! No!—the bug! It is of a brilliant gold color—with two jet black spots near one extremity of the back, and another somewhat longer, at the other. The antennæ are ——

JUPITER. Dey ain't *no* tin in him, Massa Will, I keep a-tellin' you; de bug is a goole bug, solid, ebery bit of him, inside and all, sep him wing—neber feel half so hebby a bug in my life!

LEGRAND. Well, suppose it is a gold bug, Jup, is that any reason why you shouldn't go out and get dinner ready?

JUPITER. Yes, sir, Massa Will, I'm goin' right now, sir. (*Fade out.*)

LEGRAND. (*Calls after him*) And don't let the birds burn!

JUPITER. No sir, Massa Will.

LEGRAND. The color is really almost enough to warrant Jupiter's idea of a gold bug, Friendling. You never saw a more brilliant and metallic lustre than the scales emit—but of this you cannot judge until tomorrow. In the meantime, I can give you some idea of its shape.

FRIENDLING. (*Politely interested*) Yes, please do; I shall be very interested in seeing this new gold bug of yours.

LEGRAND. Confound it, there's no paper in this desk! Never mind, I think that I have an old piece here in my pocket that will do. (*Pause.*) Ah, here it is; just pass me that pencil.

FRIENDLING. I took the liberty of starting this fire of yours, old man; hope you didn't mind?

LEGRAND. No, we need one tonight. Here, take a look at this sketch.

FRIENDLING. This heat is certainly very welcome; I'm not really thawed out yet. Just wait until I move my chair a little nearer to the grate. Now, let's see your design.

(*Pause.*)

LEGRAND. Well, what do you think of it?

FRIENDLING. This *is* a strange scarabæus, I must confess. New to me: never saw anything like it before—unless it was a skull, or a death's head—which it more nearly resembles than anything else that has come under *my* observation!

LEGRAND. A death's head!—Oh—yes—well, it has something of that appearance upon paper, no doubt. The two upper black spots look like eyes, eh? And the longer one at the bottom like a mouth—and then the shape of the whole is oval.

FRIENDLING. Perhaps so, but, Legrand, I fear that you are no artist! I must wait until I see the beetle itself, if I am to form any idea of its personal appearance.

LEGRAND. (*With a rising anger*) Well, I don't know, I draw tolerably well—*should* do so at least—have had good masters and flatter myself that I am not quite a blockhead!

FRIENDLING. But, my dear fellow, you are joking then. This is a very passable *skull*—and your beetle must be the queerest in the world if it resembles it. Where are the antennæ you spoke of?

LEGRAND. (*Thoroughly angry*) The antennæ! I am sure that you must see the antennæ! I made them as distinct as they are in the original insect, and I presume that *that* is sufficient!

FRIENDLING. (*Attempting to conciliate him*) Well, perhaps you have—still I don't see them. Here, take your drawing—I'll just wait and see the original, if you don't mind.

LEGRAND. All right, give me the paper, and wait until tomorrow! (*Pause.*) What's this—why, I didn't ——

FRIENDLING. Why, what's the matter?

LEGRAND. Oh, nothing, nothing at all —— (*To himself.*) That's very strange, very strange indeed!

(*MUSIC CUE. Theme music fades in and plays for ten seconds and then continues diminuendo underneath the dialogue of the* NARRATOR.)

www.ingramcontent.com/pod-product-compliance
Lightning Source LLC
Chambersburg PA
CBHW051437290426
44109CB00016B/1597